you're
stepping
on my
cloak and dagger

you're stepping on my cloak and dagger

ROGER HALL

NAVAL INSTITUTE PRESS
ANNAPOLIS, MARYLAND

Naval Institute Press
291 Wood Road
Annapolis, MD 21402

First Bluejacket Books printing, 2004

Library of Congress Cataloging-in-Publication Data
Hall, Roger, 1919–
        You're stepping on my cloak and dagger / Roger Hall.
        p. cm. – (Bluejacket books)
        Originally published: New York: Norton, 1957.
        ISBN 1-59114-353-5 (alk. paper)
        1. Hall, Roger, 1919– 2. United States. Office of Strategic
Services–Biography. 3. World War, 1939–1945–Personal narratives,
American. 4. World War, 1939–1945–Military intelligence–United States.
5. Intelligence officers–United States–Biography. I. Title.
II. Series.
        D810.S7H3 2004
        940.54'8673'092–dc22
        [B]

                                                        2003044276

Printed in the United States of America on acid-free paper ∞
11 10 09 08 07 06 05 04   9 8 7 6 5 4 3 2 1

Dedicated
TO
Whom it May Concern

contents

foreword   9

1. *I don my cloak*   11

2. *I get my dagger*   22

3. *an instructor's lot is not a happy one*   34

4. *don't forget to tumble*   44

5. *I am assessed*   58

6. *cops and robbers, king size*   71

7. *a Philadelphia story*   86

8. *bon voyage, indeed it was*   106

9. *RWH vs O.S.S., ETOUSA*   120

10. *they try to get even for Cornwallis*   134

11. *Lafayette, my watch was slow*   148

12. *the saints, Mr. Smith, and SHAEF*   167

13. *headquarters: seldom have so many done so much
    and accomplished less*   183

14. *Scotland and Norway*   196

15. *the decline and fall of the O.S.S.*   214

foreword

Roger Hall's *You're Stepping on My Cloak and Dagger* first appeared in 1957, and literary reviews hailed the author as one wry spy. The book, about Hall's uncommon experiences in World War II espionage, particularly captured the imagination of young readers. *Cloak and Dagger* finds Hall a real man of nerve—in both senses of the word—as he battles the enemy but more often his superiors.

Although considered a cult classic in intelligence circles, the book went out of print. Recently I discovered Hall's book, a lost gem of irresistible charm and irreverence. A sentence rarely passed without a punch line. I met with Hall and told him that many people admitted his book was the only one they had ever stolen from the library. That cheered him for hours. He had previously heard that young Central Intelligence Agency recruits were warned, book held high, "We don't want this to ever happen again." Hall loves that story and anything else that seems to confound convention. His favorite tale of wartime spying occurred in Nazi-occupied France. A colleague in the Office of Strategic Services, the wartime precursor to the CIA, had been asked to destroy a German tank sitting at a key crossroads. No one in the French Resistance could get close enough. Dressed like a French peasant and fluent in German, the OSS man approached the tank and yelled, "Mail!" When the tank lid opened, he tossed in two grenades. Mission accomplished.

OSS founder William "Wild Bill" Donovan had sought just such "glorious amateurs" for clandestine work. He was interested less in formal military expertise than in recruiting agents who could use their wits and find innovative ways, in sticky situations, to win the war. The OSS seemed an ideal match for Roger Wolcott Hall, who joked that he otherwise was destined for execution by firing squad in the regular Army.

The son of a Navy captain, Hall grew up in Annapolis with a hearty streak of patriotism but little awe of authority. To him, Admirals Chester W. Nimitz and William F. Halsey Jr. were "Uncle Chet" and "Uncle Bill." With America's entry into the war, Hall was drafted into the Army, and after going to Officer Candidate School, he became an instructor in Louisiana. An unfortunate combination of the heat, the alligators, and his natural audacity led to a series of disagreeable episodes. Enter the unsuspecting OSS.

As part of his training, Hall infiltrated a Philadelphia circuit-breaker plant by pretending to be a wounded war hero in search of work. He so impressed the firm's vice president that he not only got the job and a date with the man's daughter, but also was asked to speak at the company's war bond rally. His rousing oratory, which surprised even him, was published in a local paper. His superiors told him there was such a thing as a job too well done.

Eventually sent to England, he became an instructor again. He pleaded for commando work, but the inefficient bureaucracy worked against him. Excited about dropping into occupied France, he underwent exacting preparation and made a perfect parachute jump behind the lines. Unfortunately, they were the Allied lines. So it was back to training, next working with a group of purportedly reformed Nazis nicknamed Matthew, Mark, Simon, John, Luke, James, and Happy.

For all his misadventures, Hall wound up thriving in an organization that admired craftiness, wit, and, ultimately, confidence. When he finally arrived in a war zone, the little-known but strategic Norwegian theater of operations, he came through with flair. "Operation Better-Late-Than-Never," as he dubbed it, was a success.

Hall went on to write two novels, spent years as a freelance writer and editor, and had a stint—his favorite job—as cartoon editor for the old *True* magazine in New York. He now lives with his wife, Linda, in a Victorian-style house in Delaware's Brandywine Valley. He keeps a stash of ideas in an upstairs trunk. One is for a book called *Bayonet the Survivors and Other Love Poems*. Until Hall writes the poems, readers should be delighted to have *You're Stepping on My Cloak and Dagger* uncloaked after all these years.

Adam Bernstein
Metropolitan Staff
The Washington Post

ONE

I don my cloak

MY ORDERS were concise, with hygienic overtones:
"Report to the O.S.S. Wash."

With the inspiring words of the Commanding Officer at
Camp Plauche, Louisiana—"Never mind what I told you to
do, you do what I tell you to do!"—still ringing in my ears,
I flew to our nation's capital, found the proper building by
a process of elimination in which the Bureau of Indian Affairs was runner-up, and presented my orders to a major who
seemed supremely bored by it all.

He didn't bother to look up or return my salute. When I
started to lean on the desk and read over his shoulder he
frowned, put down the magazine, reached for my papers,
and came to life in a hurry. They were Special Orders, signed
in ink by one "George C. Marshall, Chief of Staff."

Suddenly I had found a friend. "How was your trip, Lieutenant Hall? Nice to have you with us. I think you'd better
discuss these orders with Colonel Guyon."

He led me to him personally, handling me en route like
a paper cup filled with acid. I began to wonder the minute
we walked into the Colonel's office; it must have been the
way he shook his head.

"So you're going over to the Office of Strategic Services,
son?" This in a tone of voice generally used when the parish

priest comes slowly into the death cell. Before I could answer, he asked, "Are you married, son?"

"No, sir," said I, smartly.

"None of them are," said the Colonel, mournfully.

"None of whom aren't what, sir?" I asked, not so smartly.

"None of the young officers who go over to the O.S.S. are married." These glad tidings came from the Major. Colonel Guyon shook his head again.

"No, they are all young, unmarried, junior officers." He made that combination of eight words sound like a pronouncement of doom. The conversation was terrifying me. I did what I could.

"Sir, I'm engaged."

"That doesn't count, son. Did you volunteer for this assignment?" He sounded as though he were trying to give me an out.

"Yes, sir." It was little more than a whimper.

"Well, in that case, good luck, son." He might as well have added, "There isn't any."

"Thank you, sir." I almost said "Dad."

He pulled himself together long enough to hand me a slip of paper and mumble, "Report here." I glanced at the address, it was across Constitution Avenue, a bit farther down. Trying to cheer the old boy up, I quavered, "I seem to be near you, Colonel, hope to see you again, sir."

That started him for fair. "Afraid not, Lieutenant. I've sent many a splendid young officer over there in the past two months, fine-looking fellows, and I've never seen one of them again, not one of them!"

He seemed convinced an ogre was eating those "fine-looking fellows" as fast as he sent them across the avenue. It was all too much for me. I blurted out a hasty "Thank you, Colonel Guyon," and ran.

The episode had the charm of an intermission at a wake,

and my mind began reading O.S.S. as Officers Suicide Section. I thought briefly of Aunt Louise's habit of saying, "Dear me, this is dreadful." The last time I'd heard it was at Pimlico when her choice was running last at the head of the stretch. I was thinking of horses at the time, because when death is a certainty horses and dogs are put away painlessly. Dogs are man's best friend. My best friend could put away only one thing painlessly. This involved but basically sound line of reasoning led me to one of the District of Columbia's better bars.

The soda must have dulled my senses. I became noble, and decided the least I could do was report to the organization which had rescued me from the swamps of Louisiana. That may well have been a mistake. If I hadn't reported back in '43, they probably wouldn't have missed me to this day.

The Office of Strategic Services was located midway between a brewery and a Naval hospital which catered to mental cases. During my search for Headquarters, I was thrown out of the brewery and refused admittance to the hospital. It may have been the other way around. Eventually, I wound up outside "Q" Building, one of a maze of temporary government woodpiles, some of which dated from the War of 1812.

I started up the walk, and stopped short at the sight of the largest man and the largest dog I had ever seen, apparently keeping each other at bay. The dog, a Great Dane, was lying in front of the door. The man, whose national origin wasn't obvious but who looked as though he'd come straight from Mount Olympus, was the uniformed guard on duty at the same door. Either was more than enough to keep that threshold inviolate.

I was trying vainly to find a sticking point whereon to

screw my courage when a tiny old lady trotted out the door, headed down the walk, and in passing gave the dog a solid kick in the butt.

"Move, you big ox!" The monster, which could have diced her with its tail, looked up indignantly, lumbered over to the lawn, collapsed, and went back to sleep.

If she could handle Big Ox, I figured I should at least try the guard. I went over, chattered a few inane questions, showed him the Colonel's note, and was ushered into the building. He picked up a phone, which promptly disappeared in the vastness of his mitt, and began to mutter things. Whatever went on didn't seem to make life any more bearable for him. Finally he hung up and announced that someone was coming down to collect me and take me elsewhere. I asked where. No answer, only a withering look.

I seemed to be developing a tremendous capacity for ice water, so I started down the hall toward a fountain.

"Come back here!"

He roared it rather slowly, and I slid back safely before he really finished. Then he warned me, in a deadly voice, that no one, absolutely no one, moved around "Q" Building without one of two things—an O.S.S. pass or an escort. I had only a great desire to blow the joint.

In a few moments a good-looking blonde, whose figure seemed oddly unbalanced, came around the corner. There had to be a reason for my fascinated stare, so I asked if she was an escort. She said she was, but not mine, and went over to talk to the guard. I still had designs on the water fountain, so when the lopsided charmer came past again, I humbly asked her to escort me there and back.

We went to the fountain together, came back together, somewhere along the line she mentioned owning Big Ox, and we haven't been seen together since. I never found out why her chest looked like a flight of stairs.

My escort was a long time coming, which gave me an

opportunity to drowse and reflect a bit. Things had been happening quickly of late.

It all started while I was rotting away in Louisiana, a state ideally suited for doing just that. I had been stationed at Camp Plauche, which has been conservatively described as "a place where it takes two alligators to last through the summer."

My assignment was giving basic training to Transportation Corps recruits. Being an Infantry officer, I couldn't understand why the Army Ground Forces had farmed out the cream of its March, 1943, crop sixty strong to the Army Service Forces in the first place. It didn't take me long to find out it couldn't have mattered less whether or not second lieutenants understood such things.

My weekly requests for transfer were a waste of time second to none. I'd have done as well making paper airplanes and sailing them towards Headquarters. Someone therein had dedicated his life to keeping me around. I'd come to suspect the Regimental Commander, who was queer for softball and could ill afford to lose from his team—corps champions—a left fielder who was currently hitting .375. I was tagged essential, and seemed destined to stay at least until the season ended.

Since it wasn't even half finished yet, I said, "The hell with that, and you too, sir," loudly and at regular intervals, every week end with the emphasis on late Saturday night. I finally yelled so loudly and wrote so many letters that one of the O.S.S. body snatchers got wind of my discontent.

Captain King's letter came at a time which might be called "most propitious." I had lost a fly ball in the sun, made a throwing error, and struck out three times in one game. The Regimental Commander was convinced that I'd been bought and the fix was on. He took to listening to his adjutant, Lyin' Felix, a man who earned his nickname on pure merit and no friend of mine. I seemed destined to go to the rifle range at Slidell, Louisiana, where no combination of alligators had ever been known to last past six weeks.

When word from the O.S.S. did arrive, it was along the lines of something one might hear on an "Inner Sanctum" program. "We are looking for officers who want to volunteer . . . overseas duty of a secret and highly hazardous nature . . . close combat . . . excellent physical shape and a high degree of endurance are necessary . . . background with field training . . . work that is similar to commando operations . . . fill out the enclosed forms if you are interested."

I was interested. The forms went back to Washington an hour later, special delivery airmail. I didn't lie, but I did exercise a selection of facts. That night at the Officers Club I drank a toast as best I could with crossed fingers.

Five days later I uncrossed them. My orders were on their way, in a week I was to leave Camp Plauche and report to the O.S.S. The Regimental Commander saw no point in arguing with General Marshall over the disposition of my pale white body, and in a burst of generosity occasioned by my joyfully belting a game-winning double, he gave me four days' leave, with the stipulation that I spend it in New Orleans so that I could play in one more game the day before I left.

Outside of the first letter, I didn't know what the O.S.S. was or what it did. No one at Camp Plauche had ever heard of the outfit, and my discreet inquiries produced a succession of blank looks. I reread the part about "work similar to commando operations" and decided that was a fair trade for Louisiana any day.

News of my imminent departure occasioned a display of mixed emotions among my friends. They were sorry to lose such an outstanding member of their society, but all agreed it was nicer to see me go north than into exile at Slidell, the certain alternative in case of a batting slump or sore arm.

Those last four nights I led what is known as "a full life." A compassionate God saw that the final softball game was rained out, it being an afternoon when I couldn't have hit the ground with my hat.

When it came time to pour me on the plane, everyone swarmed out to the airport. My three roommates swept all before them in their rush to reach center stage. Lieutenant Gaver was busy helping the baggage loaders. On this particular evening "coincidence" could be perfectly defined as, "the right bag getting on the right plane." Major Sweeney had clambered up on the wing of my aircraft and was giving a soul-stirring rendition of "An Arab's Farewell To His Horse," kicking vigorously at anyone who dared come near him. The poem did sound appropriate. Lieutenant Altshuler had forgotten me completely and was wandering up and down inside the plane trying to cadge a drink from the outraged passengers. He was also doing his level best to grope a lovely stewardess every time she came within reach.

For a while it was no more than an even bet I'd ever get out of New Orleans. Two worried passenger agents were scurrying around, wondering aloud if it wouldn't be wiser to keep me off the flight. The stewardess, judging me by my friends, was all for that.

In the last minutes we lured Major Sweeney off the wing and led him back to his car. He climbed in behind the wheel and sat there, tighter than an idiot's watch. His wife, slightly better off, asked, "You're not going to drive, are you?"

Sweeney thought a moment, then answered, very carefully, "I'll have to, I'm in no condition to walk."

That sent me on my way laughing. I presume the trip was uneventful, not that I'd have known otherwise, since I went out like a light bulb. By the time we landed in Washington, I was no longer a well man. Robert Benchley told all when he said the only cure for a hangover is death. As I tottered down the ramp, I would have welcomed the Dark Angel with open arms. In my pocket was the O.S.S. letter. "Volunteers must be in excellent physical shape to last through the training, which is both strenuous and hazardous. A high degree of endurance is necessary." The morning I arrived, I was hardly their boy. A hot kiss and a cold breakfast would have killed me.

These reminiscences in the "Q" Building main hall were interrupted by someone beating me about the head and shoulders. My escort had come on the scene and, for a girl, she had a good left hook. I was hurried up to the second floor, pushed through a door, and left standing in a room which seemed to be a noncommissioned officers club, first three grades only. I had never seen so many first sergeants, master sergeants, and tech sergeants as there were cluttering up that particular corner of "Q" Building. All doing nothing.

Which they continued to do. When I'm ill I don't feel well, so I picked the nearest desk, walked over to it, and asked a smug-looking master, "Sergeant, where am I and who's in charge?"

He glanced up, didn't seem to like what he saw, and answered, "This is the Registration Room, I'm in charge. Are you the guy Tiny called about?"

That did it. "On your feet, Sergeant! I am not a 'guy,' I am a lieutenant in the United States Army. I don't know or care who Tiny is, and I don't know who you are, but this I do know: One more remark such as that last one and you won't have those stripes long enough to count them!" Although my face was no more than six inches from his, I probably gave the impression of talking from a great distance. It could not have made me much beloved by all those sergeants.

"Yes, sir! Sorry, Lieutenant. Will you please have a seat and fill out these forms?"

He handed me at least twenty sheets of paper, all different. I went into them, and began to find one alarming similarity. Each wanted the name and address of person to be notified in case of death. Not a word about serious illness or injury, just death.

When I'd finished, the Sergeant, a model soldier now, took the papers, thanked me, and would the Lieutenant please sign in on the duty register and then report down the corridor to Room 2205. There was a general sigh of relief when I walked out of the zebra farm.

In Room 2205 I was met by a lieutenant with a crew cut, horn-rimmed glasses, and Westchester accent. He introduced himself.

"I'm Malcolm MacKenzie, are you Roger Hall?"

"Yes, how do you do?"

He handed me another ream of forms, and grinned as I winced. These seemed to concentrate on my educational background and what I'd done to date in the Army, rather than where to send the body in the event my religion forbade cremation. When I'd completed these, MacKenzie came back and announced we were off to see the Major.

He turned out to be a small one, with affected mannerisms and English accent to match. After giving my papers a perfunctory look, he mumbled something about, "Glad to have you with us, Hill," said "Hmmm" when MacKenzie whispered my name was Hall, then dove into a blood-chilling speech:

"You are now a member of the Office of Strategic Services. You will learn what the functions of the organization are, but for the present this will suffice. You are assigned to this branch. We are the Operational Group Command, administrative headquarters for the Operational Groups, O.G.'s for short, which are units of twenty-eight men and four officers. These units are to be parachuted deep behind enemy lines and carry out work which is designed to accomplish three things. First, organize guerrilla forces and lead them against the enemy. Second, disrupt enemy activity as much as possible. Third, send back by whatever means possible all intelligence that can be gathered. You will operate in uniform, but if you are captured, the chances are fifty to one you will not be treated as a prisoner of war. The work is highly confidential and highly dangerous. Knowing all this, do you still volunteer?"

It took him about forty seconds to deliver that little masterpiece. I thought of how much I'd love to see his face if I were to say "No." Then I thought of Nathan Hale, which didn't help a bit. I also thought of Slidell, Louisiana, and that clinched it. I said "Yes." The Major gave me a clammy handshake and turned me over to MacKenzie.

When we were alone, he asked, "What do you think of the Major?"

"He's a beauty, that one."

"Don't take him too seriously, they keep him around because he's the only one who knows that speech."

"You really ought to have someone do a follow-up on how we're going to get back from behind them there lines."

Then he began to tell me things I should know: I could tell people I was in the O.S.S. but no more; I could have my baggage sent to "Q" Building; and I was to use a Washington post-office box as my mailing address. I'd be billeted at an area, but when I asked where it was, all I got was, "We'll take you there."

The day being Thursday, I mentioned that I lived in Annapolis, thirty-six miles down the road, and how were chances of going home at noon Saturday? Mackenzie said he'd ask, and came back in a few minutes with his friendly grin and good news.

"The Colonel suggests you take off now and report back here at nine Monday morning. We'll send you to the area then."

I was at the main entrance before anyone could start asking questions about "sufficient accrued leave." The giant guard was gone, and his replacement seemed to think my honest face was enough, but Big Ox was back blocking the walk. I grabbed his collar and made him move. If I was going behind enemy lines, deep behind them, I couldn't be bothered by a dog.

Soon I'd be with my family, being feted at the Officers' Club in Annapolis. But I couldn't forget the Colonel, and the Major, and those forms. Maybe I'd been too heroic. I might become famous, someone might even write my biography, but at this point it didn't seem to be much more than an even-money bet that three important words were going to appear therein: "Ripe Old Age."

TWO

I get my dagger

IN THE quaint old village of Annapolis, Maryland, which was rapidly being stripped of most of its colonial charm by hordes of Naval Reserve officers, the family greeted me with enthusiastic, albeit slightly bewildered, shouts of welcome. My homecoming was a complete surprise, and took a bit of explaining. I told them about being in the O.S.S., which meant absolutely nothing. When I clammed up and refused to elaborate, they were worried, insulted, quizzical, and disbelieving, in that order. For the first time within memory, I wouldn't talk. They took a vote, the unanimous decision being that I was A.W.O.L. Their firm conviction that the military police would be dropping in any minute lent a not-too-quiet air of desperation to the festivities.

Dad generously offered me the car Monday morning. I got gas with some of the ration coupons I had latched onto in New Orleans by telling a naïve captain I was going to drive up to Washington, and I drove up to Washington.

My sister was horrified by these goings on, but Dad defended me by saying, "Your brother is not entirely without honor. After all, he could have sold the coupons, and besides, he left some for us."

True to his word, MacKenzie was waiting for me at Headquarters. He declined the offer of my car, and suggested I park it behind "Q" Building. Then we switched to a staff car complete with driver, and started for the area. He would talk about anything else, but not the area. He wouldn't tell where it was, what it was, or why it was. Only an ominous, "You'll find out soon enough."

I had visions of a secret flying field, a speedy trip to England, thence to the enemy lines, and beyond. But it didn't seem logical, they hadn't taught me anything. I'd blow their intelligence system beyond repair if they didn't teach me something—anything—first. I was quite ready to tell all concerned just that in the event someone started shoving.

I stopped shredding the arm rest and began to notice where we were going, or, rather, where we weren't going. I knew the District of Columbia like a lobbyist. After ten minutes of aimless cruising I realized the driver had nothing particular in mind.

On our third trip around DuPont Circle, I suggested we stop for coffee if we had all this time to kill. MacKenzie was visibly shaken, and ordered the driver to head for the area. We went all the way through the Chevy Chase section, eventually turning into River Road.

When I said, "It's lovely out this way, are we going past the Congressional Country Club?" the man almost lost his mind.

"What do you know about the Congressional Club?"

"A great deal, having spent most of my last free summer on the links or in the pool."

"You mean you've been there before?"

"Been there? Good Lord, yes, I've been there hundreds of times. Why?"

He glanced to both sides, then, pulling his head down between lifted shoulders, he whispered, "The Club is Area "F," training headquarters for the Operational Groups. You'll be doing most of your field work around there. It's supposed to simulate the conditions you'd encounter when you go into enemy territory. Our best problem area, and you probably know it like the palm of your hand."

"You mean I'll have tactical field problems on the golf course?"

"Exactly! Only there won't be any problem involved. We'll never know for sure whether or not you know what you're doing." I was afraid his concern would lead him to drastic measures.

"You gonna tell 'em?" I had a mental picture of being sent back to Louisiana, and wished I had spent that summer on Fire Island.

"No, it's no fault of yours. I knew someone would show up who knew this part of Maryland. Go through the program, try not to make it look too easy."

"Relax, I don't know the countryside that well by a long shot." This calmed him down for the time being, but he got all het up again when I forgot myself and identified an out-of-sight landmark. I kept quiet after that, but Mac obviously didn't buy it when I stared blankly out the window and asked, "Where are we?"

"About to turn into your own back yard."

Things did look familiar, in spite of some drastic changes. What had been a city block of tennis courts was now a city block of cinders and walled tents. As we went up the driveway and past the putting green, I had a flock of pleasant financial memories, but there'd be no more of that for the nonce. My erstwhile field of fortune was now the permanent landing strip for the mock-up fuselage of a C-47. Nearby hung a set of six suspended harnesses, and off to the left was a tumbling pit. The combination could mean only one thing: Parachute Training.

We entered the Club, and I moaned aloud. What had been the ballroom was now a barnlike classroom, littered with folding chairs and blackboards. The bar was still intact, but had nothing on it or behind it. The room itself had been turned into an officers lounge, with a decrepit pool table, a ping-pong table which looked as though it had been doubling as a chopping block, and too many stuffed chairs. MacKenzie sensed my dismay.

"Had to be done." He sounded sad.

The main dining room, once a place of great charm, was now a singularly unattractive G.I. mess hall. One corner had been partitioned off and screened in. It resembled a cage, and I assumed it was where the stockade prisoners ate. Later I learned there was no stockade, no prisoners, and the cage happened to be the Officers Dining Salon.

We continued our tour of the Club. The rooms upstairs were shared by the area instructorial staff and a group of wild-eyed scientists. The latter resembled cartoon characters to such a degree that I asked Mac, "What in the world are they doing here?"

"Supposed to be developing something or other."

"What?"

"I haven't the vaguest idea."

"Have they?"

"I doubt it."

A door in the hallway flew open, and a tweed-suited string-bean with the face of an intelligent squirrel politely asked, "Do either of you gentlemen have a match which I might borrow?"

Mac handed him a folder, and he ducked back into the room. Seconds later, while we were walking down the hall, there was a muffled explosion followed by some triumphant whoops. MacKenzie mused, "One of 'em must have invented something, wonder what they'll call it."

"Gunpowder."

We escaped downstairs and went to meet the staff. The Chief Instructor, a first lieutenant named Michaels, had an oafish look and an oily manner. He also had seven assistants, all second lieutenants. After a batch of rather obscure introductions, I was assigned quarters in the tents. MacKenzie made it clear I was to call him when in need, and headed back to Washington.

On the way to my tent, I turned a corner and bumped into a rugged-looking first lieutenant. The moment he said "Sorry," I knew Boston was among the cities represented. His introduction consisted of, "My name's Bob Eichler, call me Ike. Who are you?" He helped me locate my tent, then suggested we go back up to the main building for lunch.

After eating in the cage, I had another talk with Michaels. It developed that McKenzie's fears for the health and welfare of the training program were groundless, at least so far as my going through it like a streak was concerned. Having had previous experience as an instructor, I drew that duty again right off the bat. A large class of officers was headed for Area "F," and regular faculty needed whatever help was within reach. My eventual assignment was to be in the Danish Operational Group, which would organize in a month or so.

When I came out of the office, Ike was waiting to show me around the area. The first thing along his chosen route was his tent, which had several empty bunks. Ike looked at me inquiringly.

"You really want to see the area?"

"There's no hurry, it'll keep."

"What do you think of the meatball we have for a chief instructor?"

"I may kill him."

"You'll do."

The rightful owners of the bunks showed up before we could fall asleep. Ike introduced them with, "These two hoods are my closest friends, Second Lieutenant Erik Andersen and Second Lieutenant Mills Brandies." In both instances, he placed considerable emphasis on the word "Second."

Erik was a tall, blond Norwegian-American who had come

to the O.S.S. from the ski troops. Mills was a bruiser from Ohio with the body of a weight lifter and the grin of a Kewpie doll. Ike said if I wasn't going to see the area, I might as well hear about it, so the three of them had a lively discussion of my new station and its inhabitants. They made one thing abundantly clear—none of them could stand Lieutenant Michaels.

The conversation was constantly interrupted by a voice braying announcements over a loudspeaker system which blanketed the area. The program consisted, in the main, of two items: playing a recorded bugle call, and saying John Swanson was wanted in the office. I thought I knew most of the Army bugle calls, but this one had me baffled.

I finally gave up and asked, "What the hell is that call?"

"They think it's 'Officers Call,'" Erik answered, wearily, "but the Marines we have out here swear it's 'Abandon Ship.'"

"Who's John Swanson?"

"I wish to Christ I knew. That's the best-kept secret in this organization."

After what added up to nearly six months around Area "F," hearing John Swanson called an absolute minimum of fifteen times a day, I discovered he was the civilian caretaker and handyman left at the Club by its rightful owners to try and keep the place from being totally destroyed when the O.S.S. took over. He had the only complete set of keys.

The news that I could lay hands on a car, currently stashed behind "Q" Building, was greeted with howls of delight. It seemed that the social activities of my new companions had been suffering from a lack of transportation. If that was available, the rest was ready and waiting.

Waiting, I learned that very night, at The Friendly Tavern, a swinging saloon located near an immense WAVE settlement which some considerate soul had erected on the side of Washington nearest Area "F." We seldom bothered to go any farther, what with gas rationing and the certain knowledge we couldn't do much better anyway. When we weren't quaffing ale we were singing, and when we weren't doing either we were sorting out the WAVEs who kept attaching themselves to us for rations and quarters. Our group was not one to waste what spare time we could find of an evening.

But we had to be wary of questions, particularly the inevitable, "Where are you on duty?" My friends had the answer, in fact they had dozens. Erik loved to jolt people with, "We're deserters," and then try to enlist their aid in securing civilian clothes. Mills usually claimed we had returned to the States to receive multitudinous decorations, and were currently waiting to go "back over." Ike always won the prize hands down by spinning some fantastic yarn which invariably put him in the role of closing the trap on that deadliest of all German espionage agents, the infamous John Swanson. No one gave the same answer twice running, and most of our WAVE acquaintances figured us to be patients on temporary leave from the psychopathic ward at Walter Reed Hospital. We were considered nonviolent, colorful, and solvent.

This pleasant state of affairs lasted two months, and I almost enjoyed the work. It didn't take long to master the stuff I had to teach, a *soupçon* of the routine that makes guerrilla warfare thoroughly unattractive to those on the receiving end. My special babies were scouting and patrolling, and use of various infernal machines against tanks and armored vehicles. It didn't get monotonous because we were constantly improvising, and for a change of pace there were frequent sorties into Washington and its environs.

We all cast about for ways to join one of the Operational Groups in a body, but it couldn't be done. Erik was selected to lead the nonexistent Danish unit, with me as his second in command. Ike conned his way into a Greek outfit, and

Mills joined up with a French group which had lost an officer in a jeep accident. Erik and I were left with no choice but to keep instructing until someone turned up twenty-eight Danes.

I did my damndest to stay on the side of the angels, but the inevitable finally happened and I tangled with Lieutenant Michaels, thereby making a minor prophet out of practically everyone on duty at the area. It came to pass when our Chief Instructor decided I should take a class on a night compass run. This particular bunch had already been on three, and needed a fourth nearly as much as Custer needed another Indian.

At the training office, I picked up my map and the course the men were to follow by compass from point to point. It was brand-new, not the kind we could zoom around with one eye on the needle and one on the watch. It also crossed a stream I didn't remember playing in heretofore, so I asked Michaels, "Here, where we ford this creek, how deep is it, anybody know?"

"About a foot deep," he answered, adding, "I went around the course earlier this afternoon. Oh, another thing that's not on the instructor's sheet: one pin-hole flashlight for map reading. No other lights, no matches, no smoking."

"No one better wait up for us."

A night compass run through brier-patch country doesn't exactly come under the heading of "Fun in the Great Outdoors." We had a moon when we started, but by the time we came to the stream the sky had clouded over and the woods were blacker than the boots on the High Sheriff of Hell. I couldn't see the water, but I could hear it, and what I heard didn't sound "about a foot deep." I was wondering if the men would figure a way to get out of this alive when the Sergeant who had been leading the class to this point spoke up in the darkness.

"Lieutenant Hall, did you go through the Infantry School?"

"No, I went under it."

"Sir, what's the motto of the Infantry School?"

"Follow Me!" I didn't catch myself quite in time.

"Yes, sir!" It was a chorus.

"All right, you bastards, I'll send for you if it's safe."

I started to wade. Two steps later I was swimming, and not for the exercise. The stream was head high on me, and running hard enough to knock a man off his feet. The bottom was a mass of slippery rocks, and the opposite bank, about ten feet away, was a tangle of branches and vines. I was numbed by the thought of what could have so easily happened.

The rest of the class came over holding onto an improvised rope made of belts, with the smaller ones under water half the way. When the last man was across, we finished the run and headed back to the area. The men were amused, but I wasn't. Being wet and cold didn't matter, what lit my fuse was Michaels having told me that rampaging torrent was "about a foot deep." By the time we arrived back, the torrent had nothing on me.

The Chief Instructor was in the Officers Lounge, fawning over a colonel from Headquarters. I stamped in, dripping water on both of them, and opened with, "I got this way crossing that shallow stream you were telling me about. And I didn't crawl. It was six feet deep, full of slippery rocks, and running white water. We didn't have any lights, remember? I could have lost a man or several men out there with no trouble at all."

"What were you doing, Lieutenant?" the Colonel asked.

"Compass run, sir."

"And you hit a stream six feet deep," he said in a surprised tone of voice. "How wide?"

"Eight to ten feet, sir."

"Are your men all right?"

"Yes, sir."

"What about this, Lieutenant Michaels?" asked the Colonel.

"Maybe he crossed at the wrong place," said Michaels, weakly.

"We hit every other point on both sides of the stream right on the nose."

"Well, it only looked about a foot deep to me."

"Then you're a helluva judge of depth."

"Now listen, Hall—"

"You listen. If anything had happened to those men, it would have been my neck. My neck for your mistake." Looking at him, I was certain he'd never set eyes on the stream. "Don't do that to me again. And don't call me 'Hall.' It's 'Lieutenant Hall.' "

I started out of the Lounge, then remembered a slight matter of military courtesy. I turned.

"Good-night, Colonel."

"Good-night, Lieutenant Hall."

I changed uniforms and headed for The Friendly Tavern. The clan had gathered, and I told them the story. They were laughing until I reached the part about putting a verbal blast on Michaels. Then there was much speculation as to what he might do. Mills asked what my plans were, and Erik answered for me.

"Pack."

Three things combined to keep the axe from falling. Ike browsed around and found out that Michaels had never so much as set foot on the compass course complete with Swanee River, the nameless colonel who had been in the Lounge went to bat for me at Headquarters, and the large class of officers we'd been hearing about became a reality, so instructors were at a premium. I was called into the office, asked to forget past differences, and given a hearty handclasp. I spent the remainder of that morning making Erik give back the clothes and equipment he had hooked under the pretense of helping me pack.

The new officers turned out to be the pool from which the storied Jedburghs were to be selected. The Jeds were to form up into teams of three with an officer from another Allied country and a sergeant for a wireless operator. Their ultimate mission was to parachute into France and the Low Countries before D-Day to organize, arm, and, in most cases, lead the resistance forces.

When they arrived at Area "F," they were a rough-and-tumble gang of two hundred hellions, paratroopers from Fort Benning, for the most part, who had volunteered for secret missions. They didn't know the exact nature of their future assignments, and they couldn't have cared less.

There were a few goofs, misfits, and glory seekers, but once they were screened and put to work, the Jedburghs flew high. Their three prime requisites were guts, brains, and *savoir-faire*. Training them was a breeze, they did all that was expected and more with a nonchalant ease. They also did it with a flourish whenever possible, and usually with a laugh. Most of them had all the basic military stuff down cold, so the instructors were able to concentrate on the specialized hoop-la which dotted the training agenda.

The Jeds stayed three hectic weeks, and things were never quite the same after they left. Ike and Mills had moved to other areas with their respective O.G.'s, and I was beginning to suspect the mother of the Danish Group, long since known as Hamlet's Ghosts, of being barren. Erik agreed, and had himself sent to Camp Hale, Colorado, as a ski instructor with one of the O.S.S. units which had been rushed out there for training.

Area "F" suddenly lost its charm, the original gang had moved on and a flock of birdseed salesmen had moved in. I decided to check out, but they still needed instructors who knew the business, and I'd been there long enough to qualify. Getting a transfer proved difficult.

The one ray of sunshine was Captain Ralph "Moose" Elsmo, who became my closest friend. He was an ex-Norwegian O.G. officer, now on permanent limited duty because of an injury, and assigned to Headquarters. He never forgot what other personnel there too often overlooked: that they were there for the benefit of the men who were operational.

Moose was a good-natured giant with a wonderful sense of humor, a quick mind, and a fine bass voice. He loved a party, and firmly believed there are two kinds of people— those who sing and those who don't. It was a toss-up as to who admired him most, the men he commanded or his superior officers.

Another area put in a call for an instructor, and Moose saw to it that I got the assignment. MacKenzie came out to bid me farewell and assure me yet another time that the Danes were on their way. I climbed into a staff car, and found Captain Elsmo in the back seat. He'd decided to drive up to Area "B" with me, and with his usual forethought had selected a driver who sang excellent tenor. We left Area "F" on wings of song—"Bill Bailey, Won't You Please Come Home?" to be exact.

THREE

an instructor's lot is not a happy one

MY NEW station, Area "B"—the letter reputedly stood for "By God, it's a long way from nowhere"—was lost and gone up in the mountains of western Maryland. It could claim proximity to one thing, President Roosevelt's retreat, "Shangri La," which was farther up the road and considerably less accessible, being surrounded night and day by a battalion of trigger-happy Marines. They seldom fired more than twice before yelling "Halt!"

The Marines were only joshing most of the time. They knew about us and whenever we got close enough to remind them we were all on the same side, the stock answer was, "You ain't got a thing to worry about, doggie. We fired over your heads." This hardly improved anyone's peace of mind, and most of our taller men developed a posture problem.

It all went to make the field problems more realistic, though, giving new meaning to the instructor's "behind the lines" spiel. It also caused an alarming dearth of applicants for the jobs of scout or observer. I heard some touching farewells after saying, "Sergeant, send a man up that tree to have a look around." And I saw some rapid and daring descents, including high dives, at the sound of a rifle shot fired by a playful comrade.

What we wanted to do was shoot back at the Marines, firing high of course, which would most certainly have brought civil war back to the Blue Ridge Mountains. Our commanding officers couldn't quite see their way clear to declaring open season on the President's bodyguard, so we kept prowling the countryside, the Marines kept throwing lead all over the place whenever we got within an extremely variable distance they called "range," and the fact no one was sent home in a box bordered on the miraculous.

Then there was the sunny day when the President and his Secretary of State came within an instant of being mock-ambushed by one of our patrols out on a problem. A quick-thinking corporal kept his O.S.S. tigers from swarming out of the bushes and trying to stop that particular car, which is probably just as well. I doubt if the Secret Service would have asked questions first.

Such incidental spots of color were few and far between at Area "B." I had been hopelessly spoiled by Area "F" and thought my new base of operations about one-third as attractive as hell with the fires out. The rustic charm of the region made no impression.

The setup was similar to most O.S.S. training areas. Everyone bitched more because of its remote locale, but it was no different in pattern. The buildings had housed a boys' camp in happier days; now there was a permanent area detachment who wandered around under the illusion they were taking care of the place, the instructorial staff, and the student Operational Groups. Demolitions, weapons, and guerrilla warfare tactics were the order of business; the length of the course depended largely on whether or not the particular O.G. involved was slated to go boating anytime soon.

The most secluded part of the area was used as a combination staging and holding ground for groups awaiting shipment. It was no fun for those boys, spending their last days with assorted chipmunks and deer, but it couldn't be done any other way, since everything about an O.S.S. troop movement was of necessity labeled "Tippy-Top Secret."

The ones who were practically on their way envied those who were to spend yet a while in Columbia's fair domain, we envied all but them, and the Marines shot at everyone without regard for race, creed, color, or sailing date.

After five weeks without a day or night off, we suddenly found ourselves with no one to instruct. A slack period was upon us, and a welcome one at that. The Chief Instructor sent himself home on leave, leaving us to the tender mercies of Lieutenant Robelards, "Somnolent Sam" to those who knew him. He was generally acknowledged to be the most relentless horizontalist in the entire organization, but the idea of anyone sharing his life's work was abhorrent to him, so the moment he was in command he dedicated himself to keeping the rest of us busy.

The assignments Sweet Old Bobble handed to the instructors were indicative of a warped mind. The one I drew was typical—build a road. I had enough sense not to ask why, but I wanted to find out how and where, so I dropped in on Robelards.

"You really want me to build a road?"

"Yes, until we get another group up here." He was pleasant enough about it.

"How many men do I have? What do I use for equipment?"

"No men. You can have an axe, a brush hook, and a shovel."

"And where am I supposed to make this contribution to progress?"

"Start on the ridge of Scar Hill and work down."

"Fine, I can think of no place on the face of God's earth that needs a road less than Scar Hill, and I'm just the boy to build it. Thank you, and good-afternoon."

"Wait a second, Rog. You know I've got to keep the instructors busy. Besides, it's good exercise."

"I've been busy for five weeks, and I don't need exercise. Neither do the others. We need a rest."

"A rest!" His voice was brimming with indignation. "You men are in the Army. There's a war on!"

"Who told you?"

Building my road was something less than strenuous labor. I followed the line of no resistance. Testing my handiwork became the area's most popular and least approved form of divertisement. Everyone who could lay hands on a jeep would bounce up to the take-off, literally, point, and give it a whirl. I always went along to show the way, since there was none to be seen. We could, however, tell when we were running out of road: we began to hit more trees.

Another joyful feature of life at Area "B" was the calisthenics period. It was wintertime, and all the brass monkeys had left the mountains of northwest Maryland long ago in search of warmer climes, such as Finland. We'd assemble trembling in front of the main shack, then fake our way through fifteen minutes of exercise designed to improve our health. It didn't.

Robelards gave the instructions, over a microphone, from inside the shack, standing beside a glowing stove. He claimed it was too dark outside for him to read the manual, and we all knew the man lacked both the inclination and ability to memorize anything.

One of my more illustrious fellow instructors, Lieutenant Earle, took all this in a dazed stride, he being the kind who needed at least an hour to really awaken. The sight and sound of him stumbling through those "physical education" periods had me in hysterics when by all rights I should have been spitting blood. Only those nearby were fortunate enough to see his antics, but everyone in the area could hear him bewailing his fate, which he did every moment Robelards wasn't caterwauling over the loudspeaker.

Push-ups, usually the terror of any exercise session, were no more than a breather. In the predawn blackness, we'd just lie down and rest. Earle would go back to sleep in a matter of seconds if we let him, so one morning we did. He stayed right there until the sun came up. Then the Corporal of the Guard spotted him, and after a little coaching by some unprincipled lieutenants, rushed in and jarred Robelards with, "Sir, there's a body in the main driveway!"

Everyone trooped over to the scene, and all the way we kept telling Somnolent Sam his ludicrous calisthenics had finally done someone in. He damn near did all concerned in, then and there, when the corpse sat up, stretched, and said, " 'Morning, Sam. What are you doing out of bed?"

Three days later, orders arrived from Washington reassigning me to Area "F" as an instructor. Attached was a note from MacKenzie.

"They're on their way, honestly."

Which didn't leave me anywhere I wasn't two months earlier, but I was satiated with life in the mountain country, my road was built, and those Marines were bound to hit someone sooner or later. So it was back to the country club and wait for the Danes, but I was getting a bit impatient.

Outside of a brand-new set of faces on the instructorial staff, Area "F" hadn't changed. The Balkan Operational Group was now in residence; we tried to wise the boys up during the day, and ran them through their field problems at night. I crawled over every square foot of the golf course, I blew up the caddies hut until I could have planted the dummy charges in my sleep, and led ambushes against the morning milk truck with such regularity that the driver, a friendly young man named Henkensiefken who much preferred to be called Hank, on several occasions delayed his drive down River Road until I signaled that the men were properly deployed.

I spent so much time with the close-combat course of the legendary Major Fairbairn, a mild-mannered Britisher who had been Shanghai's Chief of Police and cleaned up the world's toughest gangster colony, that I was afraid to spar around with my friends for fear of maiming them. There was work to be done day and night, and the social life which had flourished during my first stretch at Area "F" was notable by its absence the second time back.

While I was frolicking around the Club, Moose and Mac-Kenzie went down to Fort Benning and became paratroopers. There was much speculation as to the reason for their drastic action, the least plausible being their desire for a break in Headquarters routine. Nobody ever convinced me it wasn't for the extra one hundred dollars they each received for being on jump duty a month.

They came back complete with boots, wings, swaggers, and many a tale of heroism and personal daring. I knew the only way I'd ever be able to drown out their noise was to go myself, then come back and outlie the pair of them. But that trip had to be postponed. Area "F" was buried under a deluge of Italian Operational Groups, and they needed instructing more than any other outfits we'd seen to date.

They were, for the most part, tough little boys from New York and Chicago, with a few real live hoods mixed in. The majority were paratroopers straight out of regular airborne divisions, and they didn't want to waste time learning things. Their one desire was to get over to the old country and start throwing knives.

So they kicked when their training program started, but they were like the Jedburghs in one respect: They had the basic military stuff in the palm of their hand, and the instructors were able to concentrate on the specialities of the house.

On night field problems, one of the most important skills was the ability to take out the sentries. No matter what attack or raid was being simulated—a radio tower, radar station, ammunition dump, or what have you—there were always sentries. These imitation enemies were portrayed by members of the Area "F" detachment.

They would go to the problem's target point, put blanks in their rifles, and do their best to spot the attackers before they could be theoretically knocked off by sentry killers. If one could get near enough to touch a sentry, or rush him before he could fire his rifle, that sentry was considered "taken out." It was fine practice, the men on guard knew what to expect, and it took a clever kid to work his way into the target without being detected.

This particular training method worked beautifully until the Italian O.G.'s arrived and brought their Latin temperaments with them. They took it so seriously and got so wrought up that by the time they had crept and crawled to the target area, they were ready to take out the sentries for fair, and they didn't care how.

On their first problem, I grabbed a brick out of a squad leader's hand just as he was about to heave it. Two nights later, another instructor got to them as they were in the final stages of pushing a dead tree over so it would knock the sentry kicking. The next night out, there was no stopping them. Three hit a guard at the same time, one dropping out of a tree, and the other two diving in from opposite sides of a path.

The instructors threatened and cajoled until they turned bright blue; the O.G.'s would be properly remorseful and mumble apologies. On the next problem they'd forget their promises to behave, sneak away from their officers and instructors, and pull something equally murderous. It was too much to ask of the area detachment, who weren't getting combat pay. Some bright soul suggested that the instructors be sentries, but cooler heads prevailed. I was so shaken by the idea that I came up with a solution.

I chose the biggest, meanest members of the Italian O.G.'s and made them sentries. Their comrades went on the muscle with them precisely once. I sat on top of the water tower and watched the internecine battle in comparative safety; only a few bodies bounced that high. From then on, the Italians took out sentries in something less than the literal sense of the phrase.

The first morning period following a night problem was devoted to a critique. This was handled by the instructor who had gone along and watched the men play the cloak-and-dagger version of Hide-and-Seek. Ordinarily, a critique was a rather dull affair, but with the Italian groups things positively sparkled.

They had tremendous pride and *esprit de corps,* and they also had thin skins. Anyone who got up on the platform and told them what they'd done wrong was wise to be careful how he did it. They'd take criticism, but not insults, real or imagined. Any instructor who crossed them in this respect lost them from that moment on.

One of the critiques I handled came after two of the groups had made a complete botch of their previous night's problem. They had been surprised, while setting up an ambush, by two armored cars. They did the right thing by blasting their way out with dummy grenades, but in the excitement only six men out of nineteen remembered to pull the pins out of their grenades. The other thirteen might as well have thrown rocks. I had to make that abundantly clear in a way they'd never forget, but not at the expense of the men who had goofed.

I rearranged the classroom for this particular critique, setting my platform and desk near a side door. On the desk I placed a grenade which had been specially doctored for the occasion. It looked real enough, but actually it was a dummy with the identifying stripes painted over. Its detonator, however, was genuine. What it amounted to was a grenade which looked and acted real until the last instant; then, instead of exploding, it popped like a firecracker.

The Italian Operational Groups marched in and took their seats. They were on edge, officers as well as men, and obviously expecting the worst. I'd gotten along fine with them during their training, but news of what had happened on the problem had spread through the area, and the working over they'd been given by the other groups had them ready to burst into flames.

I stood behind the desk watching them. Their eyes were riveted on the grenade. Then I picked it up and let them have another long look. There wasn't a sound in the room. Suddenly I pulled the pin and placed the grenade back on the desk. As I let go, the safety handle flipped off, and it started to splutter. I had five seconds.

"That, gentlemen, is how to pull the pin on a hand grenade." Three seconds. The O.G.'s were frozen in place. I counted "One" to myself, then whirled and stepped through the side door, slamming it behind me. A moment later there was a sharp "crack" in the classroom. I opened the door and stepped back behind the desk. The grenade lay there, smoke curling from the hole in the bottom where the cotton plug had blown out. The O.G.'s looked as though they were starting to breathe again, but it was still deathly quiet.

"Any questions, gentlemen?"

There were no questions, only a sudden wave of applause. They cheered, too.

The Italian Operational Groups left Area "F" shortly after my grenade lesson, and they proved to resemble the Jedburghs in still another respect: It was monstrously dull without them.

Then came the dawn. Moose came out from Washington to break the news personally.

"The plans for the Danish O.G. have folded completely."

"Oh, neat. Why?"

"Someone just got around to finding out Denmark's as flat as a pool table, there's very little natural cover, thirty-two officers and men would be lucky to last thirty-two hours."

"And it took four months to figure that out?"

"You're lucky they figured it out at all."

"So now what happens?"

"They say you're a good instructor, you can keep on doing that until something else turns up."

"Look, Moose, I'm in no big hurry to hear some German playing 'Come to Christ' on a machine gun, but I didn't hook up with Omicron Sigma Sigma to be an instructor for the duration."

"That's what I figured. You want to go to the Parachute School at Fort Benning?"

"On the other hand, good instructors are an absolute necessity in this business, and I'm one of the best."

"Not any more you're not. You'll be leaving for Benning tomorrow night."

"Wait a minute! I have to volunteer for that."

"I volunteered for you."

"Then suppose you go for me."

"I've been. Now you're going. You'll have fun jumping out of the airplanes. I'll take care of everything here and at Headquarters."

"What does that leave me to take care of?"

"Climbing down trees you didn't climb up."

FOUR

don't forget to tumble

SO I WAS forced aboard a train and headed for Columbus, Georgia. Fort Benning was no novelty to me; I had graduated from the Infantry Officers Candidate School one year ago to the very day I arrived back. I scouted around the depot and found a weapons carrier with a paratrooper leaning against it.

"How about a ride out to the Parachute School, soldier?"

"Yes, sir, that's what I'm here for. I reckon you're my only customer." He sounded disconsolate. I wondered if they paid him by the head.

After a pleasant trip through familiar territory, he dropped me in front of a group of buildings and said, "You report there, sir." He pointed vaguely at nothing in particular and drove off. Which left me with a large kit bag, a larger barracks bag, a blank look, and three copies of my orders.

Moose had taken pains to give me a generous helping of advice about the school which was destined to make the struggle easier. I had gotten in good shape on my own time, running around the golf course at Area "F" for hours on end, and doing push-ups until my arms felt like two bags full of dead mice. I figured to be ready physically.

It didn't take much time to find Headquarters, and it took even less to find out "You don't report here, Lieutenant, you

44

report to the Student Training Battalion." A truck went to
and from there twice a day; I'd just missed the first trip,
which seemed to mean a long wait. Then someone looked at
my orders, saw O.S.S. thereon, and two minutes later I was
on my way in a jeep.

The Adjutant at the student area greeted me with a cheerful, "Oh, one of the glory boys!" and proceeded to turn
me over to the Battalion Commander personally. The latter
decided the safest thing to do was get me off his hands with
all possible speed. I tried to tell the man I had six weeks,
the complete course being five, but he was in a hurry even
if I wasn't. So instead of proceeding leisurely into Class 117,
which began training in a couple of days, I was flung into
Class 116, which went into action in something less than
two hours.

The brass slammed through the necessary orders, a sergeant went over to supply and drew my equipment, a corporal filled out ninety per cent of the required forms by guess
and by God, and I took the physical exam. They should have
let me fill out the forms and sent the Corporal over to the
Infirmary, since the exam consisted of my saying, "I think
so," when a bemused medic asked me if I was in reasonably
good health.

It all got done in an unbelievable forty-five minutes. Then
the Battalion Commander grabbed my hand, wished me luck,
pushed me and my orders and my baggage and my equipment into another jeep and ordered, "Take the Lieutenant
to the Alabama area."

The Parachute School training program was divided into
four stages, each run by a captain, with a pair of lieutenants
and a dozen sergeants to help. The instructors were selected
for their over-all ability to instruct capably and ride unmerci-
fully. The time-honored punishment for any infraction of
the rules, real or imaginary, was twenty-five push-ups. Mili-

tary courtesy was faultless, and the student officers were flayed as much if not more than the student soldiers.

When my section lined up for its first formation, I got an awful shock. The battalion commander who had rushed me into this particular class had brushed aside the time-honored alphabetical scheme of things, and I was ensconced at the top of the roll. Which meant that whatever Class 116 did in the grim days ahead, "Lieutenant Hall, Roger W.," went first. Our section Sergeant knew what I was thinking.

"That's right, Lieutenant Hall, you go first all the way through, from now right through the jumps." Of all the lines and roll calls I'd endured in the Army, this was a fine time to grab front place.

"A" stage started with a roar, supplied by the instructors, and a run, supplied by the students. Not a casual trot or a brief sprint but a lung-searing shuffle which never seemed to end, and always at attention. I was never able to persuade anyone in authority that the order "Run at attention!" was a masterpiece of ambiguity. When we reached the point where we couldn't breathe anyway, we would be called upon time and again for a cadence count. That's when they started to drop.

Every time a student keeled over, an assistant instructor would be detailed to stay with him, bring him back to this world, get him back on his feet, and see that he caught up with the class. It might be three or four hours before he made it, but he'd make it, and under his own power.

Those who lasted through the run could look forward to climbing the twenty-foot ropes which seemed to hang from anything which would support the weight of a man. We were supposed to go up quickly and come down slowly. With me it worked the other way around.

Then came the Indian clubs, for which the hell with the Indians. They felt light when you picked them up, five minutes later you'd take an oath that Atlas had handed you his burden. Sooner or later—I seldom bothered to wait—you were bound to drop one or both of the clubs, which meant you had to drop down beside them—that part wasn't hard —and do push-ups. I was never able to find out whether or not that part was hard. All this time you were being taunted by an instructor, whose clubs bothered him about as much as the weight of his fingernails. His final bit of mockery was the worst.

"Anyone who wants to can throw his clubs at me, I won't duck."

He might not have known the difference between "can" and "may," but he couldn't have been safer. The clubs just slipped from our nerveless fingers. I made a concerted effort to skull him every day for a week and never hit anything but the foot of the sufferer next to me.

Then there was the sawdust pit, which sounded harmless the first time we heard about it; but after that first time, strong men paled and weak men fainted when the order was given, "To the pit with 'em!" We did exercises in the pit for fifty minutes each day, and I saw men try to crawl out when the whistle blew and not be able to drag themselves over the foot-high board at the edge. Then they'd beg their more fortunate comrades, "For God's sake, lift me out of here before the next section starts!"

The runs, the ropes, the clubs, the pit and similar niceties lasted for six days. Those who couldn't make it were weeded out, and, if they asked for it, given another chance. If a man thought he could eventually get through "A" stage, he could keep trying. One lieutenant took three shots at it before the resident psychiatrist found out he was a masochist.

We went on to "B" stage rather impressed with our newly found strength, and the instructor there straightened us out in a matter of minutes.

"You go through the Parachute School in graduated stages,

gentlemen, ostensibly designed to become increasingly difficult. Although this is the second stage, we in charge here like to think it should be the fourth. Shall we begin?" He stunned us with the way he handled the spoken word, and he proved every bit as good as his word. We slank back to our barracks at the end of the first day, and I set aside enough money to have my remains shipped home.

The pride and joy of "B" was the tower jump, the tower being forty feet straight up, with a ladder leading to a platform on top. On the way you were advised not to look down if you wanted to stay interested in your chosen profession. A cable suspended between two ex-telephone poles ran past the platform, and along this cable, which was on a slight incline, ran a wheel pulley from which was hung a parachute harness. The entire setup had all the charm of Execution Dock.

The student climbed up to the platform where an instructor was waiting, put on the harness, and took the exit position. The instructor gave the exit command sequence. When he said "Go!" and slapped the student's leg, the student lurched out in what he hoped was a proper exit, fell twenty-five feet, bounced back up ten because of the harness-and-cable combine, and then went whizzing down the cable on the pulley wheel. The ride ended when he slammed into a huge pile of sawdust thirty yards away.

My section was the first to make the tower jump, with me taking the first hop. There wasn't much to it other than a terrific psychological build up. It took a bit of nerve to step off into forty feet of nothing, but it never bothered anyone after the first time. Actually, bouncing along under the cable was good fun.

Some students hesitated, a few refused point-blank to jump. They froze in the door, and if the instructor couldn't talk them into going, their airborne days were over. That was the idea behind the tower; it got rid of the ones who could never have taken the first step, and spared them the agony of finding it out in a plane. We used to kid a lot about the tower jump, but on the second day we saw a man freeze in that platform door. Nobody laughed.

The rest of our mornings in "B" were spent learning how to handle a chute in the air, and how to land. Handling the chute wasn't difficult, and once we'd learned to drive, it wasn't hard to steer.

Learning to drive was something else. We did it the hard way, in a suspended harness which hung from wooden supports. Hanging there, a total dead weight, was brutally hard on the victim. The apparatus was affectionately known by various vulgar titles. Heart-rending indeed were the screams for mercy when someone got caught between the harness straps and a cast-iron buckle. This invariably reduced the instructors to helpless laughter, but the victim never joined in. Many a man left the suspended harness platform walking like a camel in labor.

Learning to land was a riot, nothing less. If "A" stage was supposed to make us men of iron, "B" stage seemed dedicated to the premise that iron or no, we'd break if we hit the ground hard enough. We tumbled backwards, forwards, and to both sides. We jumped, fell, dove, and were pushed off platforms ranging from three to fifteen feet in height. We came down on sawdust, dirt, canvas mats, rocks, and, as often as not, each other.

Afternoons in "B" introduced us to the gentle art of parachute packing. It was dull, but we paid close attention. You personally packed each chute you jumped, so everyone was anxious to learn. When we learned, we practiced. The chutes in the packing sheds were silk affairs which had survived one hundred jumps and then had been retired to less strenuous activity.

Class 116 got through "B" stage in fairly good shape, and wandered over to find out what "C" held in store. We knew the afternoon meant more chute packing; we soon learned the mornings meant discovering how a jump feels when you begin it halfway down.

This trick was made possible by steel towers two hundred and fifty feet high, with four arms at the top. They resembled gallows too much to suit my delicate tastes, and one of my classmates, recalling the tower jump setup, remarked, "Who the hell was the consulting architect for this place, Jack Ketch?"

An instructor heard him, and bellowed, "What was that about Jack Ketch, Lieutenant?" Then he caught me smiling, and thundered, "Lieutenant Hall, who was Jack Ketch?"

"Er—wasn't he the man who held the torch for Guy Fawkes?"

"Wrong! Give me twenty-five, sir." Then he turned to the other officer and added, "You give me twenty-five too, sir, for starting this history lesson. Ketch and Fawkes, eh. Before this week is over, we'll have you gentlemen thinking in terms of Burke and Hare." There'd been a grammarian in "B," now we had an historian in "C."

The operation of the uncontrolled descent towers was fiendishly simple. A student was harnessed into an open parachute. The rest of his section secured the outer edges of the chute to a large iron ring. The ring was then hauled to the top of the tower by a steel cable, one of which hung from each arm. The student made the trip up dangling underneath the chute-and-ring combine.

When he reached the arm, they let him hang there long enough to make his peace with God, then the chute was released from the ring, and after flapping down fifty feet, things caught hold and he floated the last two hundred in a real, live drop.

I went first, as always. There was a lively discussion among the instructors about which arm of which tower—there were four—to use. It depended on the wind, the optimistic hope being that the student would be blown away from the structure. If you started to drift toward it, you were expected to "climb your risers" and slip out of danger. We were earnestly advised to act promptly.

The staff finally decided I'd have what they kept calling "the best chance"—I loved that—on arm three of tower four. The entire class was assembled around that tower. When I realized I was being used as a demonstrator, I politely suggested one of the hired help might be better qualified. The honor remained mine.

They fastened me in the harness, my heavy-handed and light-minded fellow students fumbled around with the parachute and ring until it looked hopelessly entangled, then the order was given, "Take him up!"

I went sailing skyward on a ride which was short but interesting.

When the ring stopped, I gazed around and saw Fort Benning from a unique angle while I hung there, swinging like something on a Christmas tree. A loudspeaker blasted, "Ready, Number Three!"

I checked around to see how Number Three was getting along, and found myself quite alone. Which seemed to make me Number Three, so I answered in a small voice, "Yes."

The loudspeaker roared again.

"Sound off like a man! Are you ready, Number Three?"

I was in no mood to have some clown standing safe on earth make disparaging remarks about my formal dances, so I roared back, "You mean I have a choice? Certainly I'm ready, throw the goddam switch!"

"A simple 'Yes' will be sufficient, Lieutenant."

The ring traveled up ten more feet, there was a jolt, a drop which I felt but didn't bother to observe, and a soft "whoosh" as the chute filled out. The voice mournfully assured me I'd be dead the moment I hit the ground if I kept my present position. Then I was turned over to another voice, whose one comment was a cheery, "Feet together or broken ankles. Take your choice, sir."

My landing was adequate and little else; I got up and walked away, which is all I asked. After watching my classmates splatter themselves all over the field, I resolved to pay a little closer attention when the instructors talked about how to land. Up until the first free descent, we'd been more interested in getting out of the plane intact.

Between the towers in the morning and the packing sheds in the afternoon, "C" stage week went quickly. Any spare time was devoted to lectures. How to work your reserve chute, a comforting little thing you wore on your chest to make sure the government got a return on the money invested in your training; how to tell high-tension wires from clothes lines—"Stay clear of anything stretched between poles;" how to walk across the top of another jumper's chute in mid-air and still get down alive—"But don't be surprised if he punches you in the mouth when you're both on the ground;" in short, all the things a growing boy should know before he makes his first leap from "a plane in fright, I mean 'flight,'" to quote the number-one gag in the Parachute School's instructorial repertoire of clever sayings.

Then Friday afternoon we arrived at our packing benches and found suspiciously good-looking chutes waiting for us. The chief packer chilled our blood with, "Work carefully, gentlemen. You'll be using them Monday."

Now the first time we packed chutes we did it in about an hour. We'd been doing it every day for two weeks, and some of us had it down to twenty minutes. That afternoon, not one man left the shed in less than three hours, most of us stayed the full four, and some wanted to come back and work in the evening.

The instructors were quite familiar with such a reaction, and would have none of it. They checked the packing process at least four times, and once they said the chute was all right, you laced up the cover. Their clincher was, "It's O.K., sir, if you won't jump it, I will."

No one argued with them past that point. The only thing left to do was worry, and I swore I'd never worry about an inanimate object again the way I worried about the parachutes I packed for my first jump.

The churches did a thriving business that Sunday, the fact it was Easter giving the necessary excuse to men who hadn't been for so long they started to applaud when the choir stopped singing. And if the last day was spent in prayer, the last night was spent in retrospection. Life in the barracks wasn't exactly gay, everyone wrote at least one letter which began, "Tomorrow I make my first jump, and in case something goes wrong, I just want you to know——"

There was a negligible amount of conversation; one brief sentence per subject seemed to suffice. The usual poker game started and collapsed under the handicap of being unable to produce a dealer who could give five cards to each player each time.

A few of us, deciding that our blood spilled on the ground would be no less beneficial to the flowers for having a slight alcoholic content, made a wise move and trotted up to the Officers Club. We relaxed under the soothing influence of some good Yankee beer, and spent a far happier night than many of our brooding friends.

Next morning, breakfast was generally ignored. The company area was strangely quiet, none of the usual huzzeroo. We had acquired the reputation of being a carefree group, plenty of noise and chatter, always singing while we marched. Our repute suffered that day. Class 116 spent its prejump hours being about as colorful as a pound of flour.

They were waiting for us at the airfield. We went to our lockers with considerable misgivings and took out the chutes we'd labored over two days earlier. It was then I realized parachutes could have expressions. The small one looked smug, the big one looked sullen.

Our packing instructor came by, wished me luck, and said he wasn't worried. I profanely mentioned wishing I knew how he felt. Then we went out to the dressing benches and wrestled our way into the harness. A loudspeaker kept breaking in with uplifting gems such as, "Put 'em on right and tight, gentlemen. You're liable to go to pieces if you fall out of it eight hundred feet up. And remember this about your chutes, they're hell to clean."

After we'd waited an eternity or two in the "sweat shed," a pep talk was delivered for our edification. It ended with a completely ineffective, "Well, gentlemen, this is it!"

Some poor soul in the back benches shot his previous night's supper, and a sergeant called the roll.

"First man, first stick, plane Number One." By now I knew what to expect.

I led my stick out to the plane, got a quick but thorough check from an inspection team of instructors, then climbed into the C-47 after the men got aboard. Officers went in last and came out first. Things being in order, we took off. My seat was next to the open door, which gave me much too good a view. There wasn't much time to enjoy it though.

"Stand up!" After three weeks, it was a reflex action.

"Hook up!" Fastening my static line to the overhead cable was one part of the ceremony I handled with extreme care.

"Check your equipment!" Meaning the equipment on the front of me and the back of the man ahead. There was no one in front of me except a jumpmaster who could afford to grin because he wasn't going anywhere. I counted my chutes and smiled idiotically.

"Sound off for equipment check!" The last man started with a lusty "Twelve O.K.," and it came down the line until my "One O.K." So far as we knew, we were ready.

Then all eyes fixed on the two small lights over the door, one red the other green. The pilot turned on the red one as we neared the drop zone, and switched on the green as we passed over the drop panel. The red light came on.

"Stand in the door!" We started the chain-gang-lockstep shuffle forward. Since this was an individual exit jump, there was no hurry, certainly none on my part anyway. I swung into position, and one of the men behind me yelled, "Make it a good one, Lieutenant!"

I nodded my head with a conviction sadly lacking in my heart. Then came the jumpmaster's "Ready!" The green light flicked on, I felt a slap against my leg and heard "Go!"

My form was atrocious, about as bad as it could be considering I hadn't managed to hit the tail of the plane. I was conscious of falling forward but not downward. Then something cracked, and I was snapped like a whip. That was my introduction to the dreaded "opening shock," and it lived up to advance billing.

When I was able to tilt my head back, I checked my chute and it did look beautiful. Then I began to think about landing. There were people on the ground watching, mine being the first jump of the day, and the inevitable loudspeaker announced, "Bad exit, good recovery, you're O.K., Number One."

The last fifty feet down I concentrated on finding a soft spot, but blew that particular landscape survey completely. I hit on the bottom of a swing, and got out of it in one piece by managing a sprawling roll which combined all the best features of sliding into second base and stepping on a land mine.

Planes were dropping men all over the zone now, Class

116 was on its way. My plane made its second run, and I watched the kid who'd been sitting next to me drift in for a landing which wouldn't have broken a soap bubble.

We'd been told you could never be sure whether you were going to bounce halfway back up or ease in cotton soft. We bundled our chutes and started over to the trucks. On the way we passed a medic waving a red flag, the signal for an ambulance. Someone had broken a leg. You never knew.

On the second jump I recovered my lost form, three and four were stick jumps, crowded but without incident. We gradually got ourselves back to the point where we could pack the chutes in twenty minutes, which is more to the credit of the method used than our courage. We'd come to realize that if we did anything even approximating the correct procedure, the chute would open unless we sewed up the cover with baling wire.

Number five was the night jump, our last and qualifying descent. For a change, I jumped leading the last stick. The weather was foul, got worse, and by the time my plane took off, it was rough going around the drop zone. We went on in, there was only one stick left, and the pilot figured we'd have time to make our run.

Going into the zone, the plane behaved as a thing possessed. One jumpmaster wanted to send us out, the other thought the weather was too rocky. The pilot chimed in with the news that he'd infinitely prefer to lighten the load. The jumpmasters were still undecided. One of them asked me, "How about it, Lieutenant?"

"I'm all for getting the hell out of here. What about the men?"

"They'll follow you."

"Tell him we'll try it."

It was raining hard, and I kept my head inside, out of the slashing prop blast. The red light came on. Then there was a blinding flash of lightning, and I went out minus the green light, without ever hearing "Go!," or feeling the slap on my leg. I wanted to get into heaven while the gates were still ajar.

Once out of the plane, it was the easiest jump of them all. The lightning obligingly spotted the landing zone for me two or three times, the atmosphere was heavy because of the rain, and I came down ever so gently. I even managed to hit close to the trucks, with the landing itself being one of those cushion jobs I'd dreamed about.

As I was rolling up my chute, all the while muttering hearty self-congratulations, a voice near the trucks called, "Is Lieutenant Hall on the field?"

"Right here, Lieutenant Roger Wolcott Hall, United States Parachute Infantry!" I felt nine feet tall.

The owner of the voice came sloshing toward me. All I could make out was a trench coat and a helmet liner.

"How was the weather up there, Lieutenant?"

"Rough, very rough."

"Do you think they should have sent you out?"

"Those boys know their business."

"How was your jump?"

"Frankly, a thing of beauty. Everybody else all right?" I was in an expansive mood, and quite willing to forget past indignities.

"Yes, everyone qualified. Your class did a good job."

"You bet they did. One sixteen's a fine bunch."

"Congratulations, Lieutenant Hall." He stuck out his hand, and I shook it. "When you get back to Washington, would you give General Donovan my regards?"

"Sure will." I was still too far up in the clouds to use my head. "Regards from whom?"

"My name's Gaither. Ridgely Gaither. Good-night, Lieutenant Hall."

"Yes, sir! Thank you, sir! Good-night, sir!"

Only the commanding general of The Parachute School.

FIVE

I am assessed

I MADE IT back to "Q" Building on time and bursting with health, which seemed to surprise Moose. The inevitable followed. For one hour I discussed my trip through The Parachute School, the account being one in which the fact quotient was in inverse ratio to the difficulty of the feats of derring-do allegedly performed. The good Captain promptly counterpunched with a version of how he had gone through the same course a month or so earlier, "when it was really tough." Once again, truth was crushed to earth.

After we ran out of heroic lies, Moose brought me up to date.

"I've managed to swing a deal with 'Cozy Carl' Hoff, he's the acting branch chief over in Special Operations. They'll carry you on their roster for the time being."

"No more O.G.?"

"Not unless you want to be a professor. And incidentally, the word's around that you are impolite to chief instructors. Take my advice and change branches."

"What's Special Operations do?"

"Pretty much the same thing as the O.G.'s, only you do it on your own. You might get a radio operator if you needed one. Otherwise, it's you and the resistance groups."

"All sounds very interesting. I quit."

"Another thing, Cozy Carl wants you to get an 'S' Report.

Bring back a good one and you'll be permanently assigned to S.O."

Again Moose filled in the gaps. The O.S.S. had gotten around to setting up an assessment school, which was called Area "S" for no particular reason, unless it was because there are four "s's" in "assess." You went there, stayed three days, took all manner of tests—physical, mental, and moral—then the school powers made out your "S" Report and sent it back to Washington.

An "S" Report was terribly top secret. It said what was wrong with you, and what was right. Whether or not you should be kept in the O.S.S., whether or not you should be sent overseas, and, if so, what duty you should perform once you got there. Headquarters placed what bordered on blind faith in the reports; once the area got underway, it was virtually impossible to be sent overseas without a favorable nod from "S." This was frequently offered as an explanation for the quality of the personnel on duty in Washington.

By the time they got around to assaying me, I had been in the cloak-and-dagger business a mere seven months, and had seen plenty of dagger (rubber) but not much cloak. Now it started. Everything about Area "S" was very sneaky, even going down there.

First, I was called into my branch office and given a numbing security lecture. Then, after I seemed properly convinced that the whole thing was a big secret, they gave me a phoney name. Any name—I could pick it—but it had to be acceptable to them. I knew they wouldn't let me go as Student Michaels Is A Horse's Ass no matter how hard I leaned on my Mohawk Indian ancestry, so I borrowed the nickname of the late "Cobber" Cain, an Australian pilot who had been top ace in the R.A.F. deck at the time of his death, and went into the record books as Student Cobber.

I was told to report at eight the next morning, complete with toilet articles and a clear mind. I would then change into fatigue clothes. The rest of the class going down to be assessed would do the same, we'd all pile into a truck, and it would take us to the area.

The idea of changing into fatigues was to destroy what was left of your identity. Your name was gone; if you had a uniform and rank or grade, they went too. If you were a civilian, no one could tell by looking. The clothing change was made in strict privacy; your classmates didn't see you until after the switch.

The most important link in the no-identity chain was known as a "cover story," that being any plausible tale except the truth about who, what, how, and why you were. The prime object at most O.S.S. schools and areas catering to "special bodies" was to break the other fellow's "cover."

I thought a small head start in that direction might not be a bad idea, so I arrived in front of the designated building early and sat on a bench across the street, trying to figure out who were going to be my school chums. Most of them were agonizingly casual about things, and consequently easy to spot.

I went in to report, got shuffled around through a maze of corridors which would have disturbed a case-hardened Harvard rat, and ended up in a dressing booth with an armful of fatigue clothes. I climbed into them, handed my beloved boots and uniform and university ring to a corporal who was to be their guardian, and went out to meet the others.

They were a nondescript crew at best, and the fatigues didn't help. I had a feeling the O.S.S. wasn't going to hatch many hitters out of this clutch of eggs. There were nineteen all told, in a complete assortment of ages, shapes, and sizes.

It took an uncomfortable hour in the back of a truck to get to Area "S," but the ride was forgotten as soon as we saw the place. It gave every evidence of having been a gentleman farmer's estate, and whoever he was, he knew how to live.

We pulled up in front of the mansion, jumped out, and were immediately set upon by several large dogs. The brutes were being playful and probably didn't know they could maim by sheer impact. Some of our less intrepid members climbed right back in the truck.

I stood my ground, flanked by two new friends, Student Bucephalus and Student Hercules. Behind the dogs came what we assumed to be the staff. They turned out to be professors, doctors, assistants, psychologists, psychiatrists, and representatives of various allied arts. Their mission was to examine and test us in every way known to man. We were all impressed by their appearance, I had never seen so much radiant good cheer. Bucephalus took one look and muttered, "Oh my God, the happiness boys!" The name stuck. Whatever they did to us, the boys did all they could for us.

We were dragged inside by the beamish ones, shown to our quarters, given a rough idea of what to expect in the next three days, and turned loose for an hour. Hercules and Bucephalus started bickering good-naturedly.

"Look, I don't want to break your cover, which would be simple enough to do because you're so dumb, but I might find out you're in our Army, and that would destroy my morale. I would like to know one thing, where did you get the silly name?"

"And you call me dumb. Cobber, tell him who Bucephalus was."

"Well, here goes my cover. Bucephalus was the horse ridden by my former commanding officer, Alexander the Great."

"Right. Hercules, I think we'll change your name. Herky-Jerky. No. Jerk. No. Stupid. That's it! Student Stupid! Perfect!" He rushed off to notify the staff.

Next order of business was a meeting at which the class formally met the staff and each other. As this began, four young ladies entered the room. One of them, a redhead, was a real looker, and we were delighted to learn they were also in the class, having been brought down in a separate car. Some wise soul knew it wouldn't have been fair to throw them in the back of that truck.

Our trio staked a claim on the redhead, labeled her "Flame," and snarled at anyone who came near. We never really had a chance though, the girls were only around for twenty-four hours.

Then it hit us. We were tested morning, noon, afternoon, and most of the night. Every conceivable way. Oral, written, drawn, checked, guessed, and figured. We filled in blanks, picked numbers, chose pictures, pulled levers, pushed buttons, and wrote page after page.

We did real problems in the field, and we did imaginary problems in the house. We played Cops and Robbers, Cowboys and Indians, and Pussy Wants A Corner. We hunted and were hunted. We ran a treasure hunt around an obstacle hunt against the clock. We were given five minutes to search an innocuous-looking room, and ten minutes to write a detailed description of its recent occupant. Bucephalus found a blonde wig and a hollow needle, and promptly pegged the inhabitant "a transvestite junkie."

All the tests were individual affairs, what you did at "S" you did strictly on your own hook. One little dandy, unofficially called The Temper Tester, involved building a wooden cage big enough to hold a man. The instructor gave you the plans, a collection of blocks and rods which resembled an oversize Tinker Toy set, and two assistants. The catch was that the assistants weren't there to assist. Anything but.

You didn't know it, and the instructor sat in a corner, noting how you reacted. Giving orders to the "helpers" did less than no good. All they had in mind was keeping you from putting the cage together. They were subtle, and many a student blew his bonnet before the allotted fifteen minutes passed. Things reached the physical violence stage frequently —the instructor was supposed to step in and prevent that —but one particularly short-tempered individual flattened all three plotters before an explanation was possible.

In spite of bribes, soft soap, appeals to reason, attempted beatings, horrible threats, and every other trick the students could conjure up, the cage was never completely assembled. Least of all by me. After watching those two kick my work apart once, and fall through it the next time, I realized I was being had, gave up quietly, and spent the remaining time trying to interest the unholy three in a black market whisky-buying deal I dreamed up on the spot.

The roughest test came late the second night, when everyone was dead tired, and, as always, we took it one by one. The hypothetical situation was that you had been nabbed while going through top-secret files in the War Department, caught so red-handed a real alibi was out of the question. The police had brought you before a three-man investigation board. You were told all this precisely three minutes before going into the interrogation room. You were also told your final "S" Report rating depended on whether or not you could talk your way out.

You hardly had time to think before an instructor said, "All right, they're ready for you. Remember, you can't feign amnesia or insanity, and you can't refuse to talk. Don't try to be cute, everything depends on how you make out in there. Good luck."

I tried being stupid, which was exactly how I felt, and it didn't even come close to working. They tore my story apart in a matter of minutes and were plenty tough about it in the process. Students often broke down completely under the verbal beating those three handed out.

They belted me with, "You didn't blunder into the wrong

office, Mister Cobber, you blundered into the wrong organization. We can't use you in the O.S.S."

I was sent into another room and left alone to wonder how I was going to explain things to my father and Moose and Erik. All I could hope was that Camp Plauche had sunk back into the swamps, or that maybe I could go back to Fort Benning and get in an airborne outfit. In came another instructor, one of my favorites.

"Hello, Cobber, how'd you make out?"

"I blew it."

"Oh, I am sorry to hear that. And you were doing so well, too. Cigarette?"

"Thanks. What happens now?"

"Well, I'm afraid they'll send you back to Washington, then to an officers replacement depot."

"Jesus, I could do without that."

"Maybe you can get sent back to your old outfit."

"I could do without that, too."

"Maybe they'll give you some leave, at least you'll get a delay en route. So you'll see your family."

"What'll I tell them? What'll I tell my friends? That I'm too goddamn stupid to make it in the O.S.S.? I know branch chiefs who can't compute simple interest. And I get bounced!"

"It's rough, I know. Wish I could help you, but you'll get along all right. This war can't last forever, when it's over we'll all pick up where we left off. I can get my Master's; what'll you do, go back to college?"

"I hope I live to see that day."

"You will. Where'd you go?"

"University of—," and right there something clicked. This nice man was asking too many questions. It was only by the grace of God I hadn't blurted out that my old outfit was in Louisiana, my family was in Annapolis, and I'd gone to the University of Virginia. Any of those answers would have busted my cover story to bits. Maybe I was on my way out of the O.S.S., but I hadn't seen the orders yet. I looked at my "favorite instructor" and smiled.

"I'm from the Seventh Division. My family lives in New York. I went to the University of North Carolina. What are you selling, smooth boy?"

"Nothing, Cobber." He sounded hurt. "I thought maybe you'd feel better if we talked."

"I'll feel better if you're a little less inquisitive."

"Nice work, Cobber, nice work." He sounded quite pleased now. "I didn't think we'd trip you. Not with that suspicious nature of yours."

"Meaning?"

"It's a sweetness-and-light routine, we want to find out how a student reacts when the tension eases, whether you talk too much when you relax. Most of all, whether you maintain your 'cover.'"

"And those three bastards who wrecked me?"

"Just softening you up for me."

"You're despicable." We were both smiling now.

"Part of my charm."

"What if I'd spilled my guts?"

"Doesn't make much difference if the rest of the work has been satisfactory. We're not trying to crucify anyone, just make sure they don't do it again."

"You'll never know how close you came to knocking me over."

"Coming close doesn't count in this business. Time for me to take on the next one. See you tomorrow." I started out of the room and he spoke again.

"University of North Carolina, huh?"

"Yes."

"Funny, I went to law school at the University of Virginia. Could have sworn I saw you down there."

That test drove home the fact that you had to stay ready all day every day. The staff and your classmates were always trying to break through your precious cover, and any time you got a pat on the back, someone was just feeling for a soft spot to slip in a big, long stabber.

This sort of thing went on all the time. The strain was hardly unbearable, but we felt it. Most of the students felt it more than my two friends and I. We managed to bend a part of each day's agenda slightly out of shape. Not that we let our irreverence get out of hand, we all knew the value of a good "S" Report.

The three days we were on trial included two hours with a psychiatrist. This was the only time we were under orders to tell the truth, our stories being strictly between ourselves and the Doc. He used it to make up his little part of the over-all stew from which the final report was prepared.

Only I drew a lady wig picker. Fortyish, attractive, with what I took to be a Viennese accent, and extremely sharp. We got along famously together. I was so delighted to be able to tell the whole truth again, it being practically alien to me by then, that I rattled along for one hundred and fifteen minutes.

By the end of the third day, the staff knew all they wanted to know, which was fortunate, since the class was orry-eyed from all the tests. So they wound things up with a party. Hercules and I were playing a delightful parlor game which involved knocking a small wooden ball into a cage with a series of paddles fastened on twirling sticks. We'd been playing every spare minute we could find, and this was the championship match. Bucephalus insisted on being the referee, a job he fulfilled with stupefying incompetence, all the while reminding us, "I can be bought."

In the midst of a furious exchange, we heard glasses tinkling and bottles banging. The staff paraded into the recreation room bearing booze, ice, and glasses. While Hercules stood there, stunned, I slammed home the winning shot, and headed

for where I thought they'd set up the bar, his howls of pro-
test ringing in my ears.

"This is a farewell party, given by the staff for the class,"
said one of the instructors.

"How very nice," said I, grabbing a fifth of Scotch.

We settled down, the Director made a brief and charming
speech, telling us we had been an excellent group, we'd done
well, and we'd earned a little relaxation, so go to it. We went,
and in less than an hour, a goodly number of my comrades
fell slightly drunk. The staff was lapping it up with us, and
chatting merrily with everyone. Then one of the instructors
casually asked, "What do you think we should do with the
hard-core Nazis after the war?"

This started a general discussion, with the staff leading the
way. Then members of the class arose, most of them swaying
a bit, and delivered themselves of various opinions. Argu-
ments started, theories were expounded. My friends and I
were off in a corner, listening to the alcoholic chatter and
keeping quiet for a change. It must have dawned on all three
of us at the same time. I nudged Bucephalus.

"This whole deal is as queer as a Chinese flag. Most of the
class is fractured, but every man on the staff is cold sober.
It's a fix."

"I was just noticing that. They're all drinking out of the
same bottles, too, must be tea. Why those foxy bastards,"
he said admiringly. "This is no party, it's as much a test as
anything else has been."

"I been waiting for you guys to realize it," said Hercules.
"They want to know how we handle ourselves after gazing
upon the wine while it is red."

"Then you'd better hurry up and get loaded," I told him.
"You're a total failure this way."

The "what to do with the hard-core Nazis" debate was in
high gear now. Some of the talk was intelligent, some was
largely unintelligible, some showed the liquor had dulled

the speaker's mind to the point where he was likely to say anything. I counted seven cover stories which were blown sky high. The staff took it all in. They also noted the way we were staying out of things, which was highly unusual. One of them asked, "How do you feel about this, Hercules?"

Our boy hauled himself erect, but before he could answer, Bucephalus muttered, "Now for Christ's sake don't embarrass us by admitting you don't know what 'hard core' means." Hercules went right back down, roaring.

Before they could come after us again, a student leaped to his feet shouting, "Castrate 'em all in the morning." He then fell flat on the floor, evidently gathering strength for his next address. While they were lifting him into a chair, Hercules giggled, "I don't wanna talk about large-bore Nazis. Let's sing."

This seemed a splendid idea, so we launched into "On-ward, Christian Soldiers," substituting freely in the lyrics, "conscript" for "Christian" being particularly well received. The Director made a final, direct plea.

"Aren't you fellows going to enter into this discussion at all?" Hercules finished that angle forever by insisting on absolute quiet while he sang something he devoutly described as "my mother's favorite hymn."

> "I am Jesus' little lamb.
> He has made me what I am.
> He will wash me white as snow.
> What a dirty little job for Jesus!"

Everyone collapsed, and the staff gave up. The happiness boys had evidently ascertained the liquor reaction of every-one but us, and since ours was apparently not to be had, they broke down and got blind for real.

Later, much later, we adopted the Director, who finally

had to be led upstairs happily singing our newest song, "Oh, God bless you and keep you, Mata Machree!"

We tried the paddle game once more, but the contest ended abruptly when the referee fell through the table. It was obviously time for bed, so we ricocheted upstairs to our room, with Hercules bringing along three empty bottles under the mistaken notion that they were dear friends who had gone on to bliss eternal.

"And I was with them when they died," he announced reverently.

Next day, those of the staff who could navigate came out to wish us Godspeed. We caught a brief glimpse of the Director waving feebly from an upstairs window, and Hercules asked, "Was he that color last night?"

After the trip to Headquarters, we reclaimed our clothes and identity in the same sneaky way we'd given them up, and were turned loose. My friends and I met around the corner; Bucephalus turned out to be a lieutenant colonel in the Field Artillery, Hercules a lieutenant colonel in the Engineers. Both wore parachute wings. Their mutual dismay when each saw the other's silver oak leaves seemed to make them overlook my lowly status. They had orders to leave for another area immediately, so I saw them off. As their staff car drove away, they were still at it. The last words I heard were, "Wait a minute, Colonel, what's your date of rank?"

One thing I knew, my "S" Report was back in Washington by now, and I wouldn't have long to wonder. Moose was at his desk when I walked in.

"Welcome home, how'd it go?"

"All right, I think. Any official verdict yet?"

"I'll go down and ask the Colonel. Wait here."

He wasn't gone long, and when he ambled back, one look was enough.

"Nice work, your report was excellent."

"Now what?"

"You can practically call your own shot. You're a qualified parachutist, you've had a good hunk of O.S.S. training, and your "S" Report fairly glistens. You can probably stay in Special Operations, or go into either Secret Intelligence or Marine Intelligence. I wonder what Cozy Carl thinks about this. I'll give him a ring. Wait in the other office a second."

He came out five minutes later with a hard look on his face, and said, "Lieutenant Colonel Hoff saw your 'S' Report before anyone else did. Orders have already been cut assigning you to S.O. on a permanent status. Now you know why they call him Cozy Carl; he bets on races after they're run."

It didn't bother me, though. I was now the property of Special Operations, and they had a reputation of being good to the help. I was tabbed for overseas duty as soon as a slot opened up in the European Theater. Until then, I was given permission to live in Washington if I so desired. I did.

To top it all, Erik the Great came barreling back from Camp Hale. He admitted his most outstanding bit of instructing was to take the best-looking WAC on the post out for a ski lesson and break her leg.

"Lovely girl," he said, "but a bit clumsy."

SIX

cops and robbers, king size

ROAMING around unleashed wore thin much more quickly than anticipated. In less than a week I went up to the branch office and asked the head of my section if I could trot away to school and make a little more advantageous use of all the time on my hands. There were several O.S.S. institutions of higher learning within reach, and since I had been told I wouldn't be going overseas for at least another month, I asked to be sent to one.

My request wound up on the desk of a rather slow-witted Marine captain. The news that I wanted to do something came to him as a profound shock. His first remark was typical.

"Are you in some kind of trouble?"

"Not yet, sir, but I'm likely to be soon if I keep hanging around this laughing academy with nothing to do."

After a bit of wrangling, I convinced the man that my intentions were honorable. He was overwhelmed to the point where he outdid himself and made arrangements for me to go up to Area "E," romantically and erroneously called "The Spy School."

This area didn't turn out the finished product; you didn't send them a man and get back a spy. It taught the basic fundamentals, and was designed primarily to find out if a student was worth further training. He learned a great deal about becoming an agent in the process, and practiced what he learned on actual problems, but no one went from Area "E" into the real thing.

He was first sent to the advanced schools, almost all of which were located overseas in the theater of operations involved. There he got the authentic agent instruction. Area "E" was excellent as far as it went, which was not much past kindergarten when it came to espionage education.

I was delighted at the idea of going there, but I knew perfectly well I wasn't going to be a secret agent anytime soon—not unless some theater intelligence chief would settle for a deaf mute. I could get by in French, but as for passing as a native of la belle France, I'd have done just as well pretending I was one of her Senegalese sons. So I went to Area "E" hoping that whatever I happened to learn might come in handy sometime, somewhere.

Getting ready to go was complicated. The trip called for civilian clothes, which sent me hurrying to Annapolis. The sight of me heisting a dozen of my father's white shirts and changing into mufti sent the family into consultation. This time they decided I'd deserted, and voted practically unanimously to stick by me. The only dissenting ballot was cast by our cook, whose patriotism knew no bounds. She was all for turning me in.

Getting to Area "S" had been slinky enough, going to "E" was twice that and carry two. First, I had to have a false name. Having done well with Cobber, I chose it again. Second, there was a sealed envelope to be opened at eight sharp the next morning, with me dressed and ready to skip town. Third, an absolutely airtight cover. Getting one was no problem, keeping it for a month with everyone between here and there trying to break through it was something else.

I planned to get a good night's rest so the sealed envelope and I would be on reading terms in the morning. It was not to be. Erik knocked the door down and dragged me away to what started out as a perfectly nice party, degenerated into something less, and wound up displaying all the least admirable features of a medieval boar hunt. I lasted just long enough to leave word with the switchboard operator.

"This is Lieutenant Hall, please call me at seven in the morning."

"Yes, sir, good night."

"And again at seven-fifteen."

"Yes, sir, good night."

"And again at seven-thirty."

"Yes, Lieutenant. What would you like us to do then, blast?"

They did have to send someone up to knock on the door at seven-thirty; the second time the phone rang I disconnected it the hard way. The knocking finally awakened me, but that was only half the battle. I was in grand condition to start training. The only part about being a spy which interested me was the prospect of being executed by a firing squad.

I read my instructions after tearing the envelope open and the enclosed letter in half with one trembling gesture. It was terse, which was fortunate. I was to go to Baltimore, be there by eleven in the morning, walk from the Penn Station to the Mount Royal Hotel, find a black Buick sedan with Maryland license plate so-and-so, ask the driver if he was Doctor Baxter, and he would be. From then on I was in his hands.

I was to maintain my cover at all times, act normally, and not get picked up. If I did get into trouble, I was to talk my way out of it. If things became completely unmanageable, there was a phone number to call, but it was to be used only after all else had failed. I sneered at the thought. They'd never take me alive. Feeling the way I did, it was an even-money bet.

A carefully selected and cautiously eaten breakfast, followed by a leisurely stroll to the station, restored my health.

Once on board the train, I amused myself by trying to spot other members of the class headed for Area "E." I was sure some of them must be going over with me. There were two fine prospects in the car. One was making a singularly unconvincing attempt to appear terribly casual, the other gave the impression of having recently committed murder. I began to stare, first at one, then the other.

Whenever either looked up, I'd fix him with a suspicious glare. The murderer actually began to sweat, so I stopped bothering him, but the actor became worse by the minute. I was mulling over a plan to frighten him to death when I realized I might be looking just as ridiculous to some unknown student who might have me spotted. I was feeling properly contrite when a good-looking, well-dressed young man slid into the seat beside me. He smiled, nodded, and said two words.

"Hi, spy."

I fought back a desire to dive through the window, remained magnificently cool, and asked, "I beg your pardon?"

"I said 'Hi, spy.' It's not too good, is it? Well, anyway, you're going to Area 'E' and so am I. My name's Student Gordon, what's yours?"

They weren't going to knock me out of it that fast.

"I'm afraid I don't know what you're talking about, Mr. Gordon. I'm going to New York, not Area 'E,' wherever that may be. If it'll make you any happier to know my name, it's Robert Hawthorne." This guy wanted a cover story, he was going to get mine with a lace border. I waited for his next lead.

"If you want to play games, all right. I thought you might remember meeting me at that party last night in the Statler. You were a paratroop lieutenant then, you're in civvies now. You're in the O.S.S., and I'll bet you're meeting a Doctor Baxter in Baltimore. I honestly don't remember your real name, so you can stop worrying about that."

All this in a properly low voice. I had to grin back at him. Twenty minutes out of Washington and I was deep in con-- versation with another student, which was strictly against the rules.

"You win, master mind. I'm Student Cobber." We shook hands, and were firm friends by the time the train arrived in Baltimore.

We parted company in front of the station, and five min- utes later greeted each other effusively in front of the Mount Royal Hotel, which was complete with the black Buick sedan, Doctor Baxter, the actor, the murderer, and a third young man who looked far more capable than the other three put together.

Gordon greeted the Doctor with a hearty, "Hello Baxter, you old quack, I hear they suspended your license. Well, you can't save 'em all. Don't remember me, eh? Name's Gordon. This is my friend, Cobber. He's a mental case, but only occasionally violent."

We piled into the Buick, chattering merrily and not bother- ing to explain how we'd come to know each other. Doctor Baxter—I won a dollar from Gordon betting he'd turn out to be a corporal—got in behind the wheel, ignored Gordon's polite, "Would you like me to drive?" and started us off on the first leg of our perilous journey.

The area turned out to be near Cockeysville, a somewhat remote hamlet in my native state of Maryland. On the way, Gordon and I tried to talk to the others, but quickly gave up on the actor and the murderer. The third student, he who looked capable, introduced himself as Student Mitch, and fitted into our company nicely.

"E" was another country estate, larger and more sprawling than "S," but not as nice. There was no triumphal entry this time. One rather forlorn individual met us at the door, led us inside, then up to our rooms. The rest of the class had

arrived ahead of us. They were sitting around downstairs staring self-consciously at the floor. By the time we had unpacked
and joined them, the Chief Instructor was on the scene.

Captain Ezra Shine proved to be a sharp article. After a
speech of welcome, he told us about the area, what we could
expect, and what was expected of us. He also cleared up
any illusions we might have had about being made into
agents in thirty days.

"Although some of you may have doubts about pursuing
this line of endeavor any further than that, let me assure you
it could happen. You wouldn't be here if such a possibility
didn't exist. So it is absolutely imperative you maintain your
covers at all times and at all costs." I was wondering just how
well I could learn to speak a foreign language in a month
when the Captain began to call the class roll.

He rattled off names such as Dusty, Bob, Earl, Raymond,
and Homer. Then came an original one—Ossian. It belonged
to a little fellow of about forty with the manner of a gentleman and the looks of a cross between Roland Young and the
White Rabbit. Mitch, Gordon, and I decided to throw in with
him on the spot.

The Captain read on down the list, with the individual
members rising to be introduced.

"Student Cobber."

"Sir." It hardly seemed necessary to say "here."

"Ah yes, Cobber. You have been chosen class leader and
will be in charge of your twenty-one mates for the next
month. Don't look so horrified; it won't be that bad."

I was too stunned to say anything, but Mitch mournfully
informed Gordon, "We've cast our lot with a copper's nark."

After the roll call and introductions, we met the Captain
privately in his office. The purpose was to go over our cover
stories with him. If he didn't like them, or could find flaws
in them, they had to be changed. After pleading in vain to
get out of the class leader assignment, I gave him my story.

Robert Hawthorne, age twenty-three, single, born and educated in New Orleans, former captain in the paratroops, injured in the North African jump, medically discharged from the Army, now located in Washington trying to get a job with the State Department. The narrative was complete with facts, names, and dates. He picked at it awhile, I knew the answers, and he said it would do.

"It would seem I have made a fortunate choice," he said, leaning back in his chair and lighting a cigarette. "A former paratrooper captain should make a fine class leader."

"Sir, the time has come to tell the truth," said I, determined to lie my way out if possible. "The only thing I've ever commanded was the awkward squad in a C.C.C. camp."

"Not if you're twenty-three you didn't. Ask the next student to come in, will you?" He was not to be denied.

Things started the next morning. We drew fatigues to work in and half a dozen textbooks. Our first class was radio, so we took an aptitude test for sending and receiving Morse code. The schedule called for an hour of radio every day, the object being to learn how to send and receive a minimum of five words a minute. I marked up the highest aptitude grade in the class, but the day I left "E" I could send two words a minute and receive three. Everyone else was running ten and fifteen with no trouble at all. The "ditty dah dit" business was quite beyond me.

Another hour each day dealt with a different kind of code, cryptography. It was fascinating, but too much at a crack left the mind fuzzy. After the class period we had homework—digging a message out of a code, or putting one into a code. We learned two master systems, both depending on a set of key words which could be changed as often as necessary. Properly used, they were as close to being unbreakable as codes could be.

Knowing the way the code worked didn't help unless you knew the key word arrangement, too. We caught on to the codes in three days; the rest of the time we fractured our brains trying to figure out messages in which there were intentional mistakes.

It involved all the niceties of doing analytical calculus, estimating the corporate income tax for General Motors, and picking a good thing in the fifth race at Belmont Park. The instructor was a kind, patient, and brilliant man. The fact that the entire class ended up knowing how to handle those codes was a tribute to his teaching genius rather than to our ability to grasp. The last few minutes of every cryptography class found the air thick with two things, flying code pads and enraged screams of "To hell with it, I'll send the son-of-a-bitch straight!"

We had seemingly endless hours of indoor class work, most of it listening to lectures or watching films. We learned police methods, Gestapo methods, S.S. methods, Japanese Secret Service methods, and Italian Carabinieri methods. There was an extensive course in body search, then an even longer one in how to hide something in or on your own body. How to search a room, then how to conceal something in the same room. How to tap a phone, how to know if one was tapped. How to rig up a dictaphone from a regular telephone, and how to plant it. How to steal anything you could lift, how to open letters and reseal them. How to tail someone through hell and high water, how to get rid of someone tailing you. How to break into practically anything anywhere and get out again leaving the place looking untouched.

There was an excellent course on lock picking, another on how to make and use skeleton keys. We learned how to use secret writing, and how to detect it. How to interrogate a person, and how to trick him into revealing things. How to maintain cover, and the hundreds of ways it could be broken. How to pass messages over the phone or by hand. The best way to carry secret documents, the best way to take them from someone else.

In the rough-stuff department, how to kill with a small rock, a pencil, or even a folded newspaper. How to act in enemy territory, how to avoid checks and searches. Yet all we learned was no more than a fraction of what a man or woman had to know in order to stay alive one day where it counted. An "E" student was jack-of-all agent trades but master of none. They might make a master of him later on.

We had our share of outdoor work, too, much of it a carbon copy of what I'd taught at Areas "F" and "B." One new twist was learning how to milk a cow—we damn near pulled the poor animal apart—another was learning how to drive various foreign cars. Since my cover included three heroic years in the Army, I could claim knowledge of most of the outdoor work. This was designed to get me some time off, but it boomeranged. Captain Shine promptly made me an assistant instructor in all phases of training which were military or paramilitary in nature.

When it came to the special equipment and secret weapons, I wasn't much help, and I was less when they brought out the specialized demolitions equipment. There were exploding fountain pens, incendiary bombs which looked and wrote like mechanical pencils, and plastic explosive which looked, felt, smelled, tasted, and behaved as though it were modeling clay—until you stuck a fuse and detonator in it.

The pens, pencils, and modeling clay were only three of literally dozens of gadgets which had been invented and expanded by the Research and Development Branch of the O.S.S. Most of them were hellishly clever, and all were effective. It got to the point where we expected anything in the area to blow up or burst into flames.

The "break-cover" game went on day and night. I didn't trust anyone, least of all Mitch, Gordon, and Ossian. They returned the compliment. My luggage was searched and handled so often it began to wear out. I left the locks open to save them from the ravages of twenty-one amateur Raffles.

It was wise to think carefully before answering even the most innocuous question. The best way to do it was to stall by countering in turn with another question. That could be taken to some fairly ridiculous extremes, though.

"What time is it?"

"What does your watch say?"

The big event was when the mail arrived each day at noon. They sent it up from Washington with the real names covered by thick black crayon marks, and the student names written in pencil. Once the letters were passed out, the party started.

To lessen physical violence, there were certain parts of the house and grounds known as "safe areas." While you were in one of these, you could read your mail and no one was allowed to walk up, hit you over the head with a chair, and steal your envelopes. Outside of these safe areas, anything went and often did. If you kept your mail after reading it, you risked having it stolen or simply taken by force.

Once they got the envelope, it was a simple matter to soak off the black crayon, and there went the most important part of your cover. None of this disturbed me; I didn't get much mail, and what I did receive I burned after one quick reading. On the rare occasions when I did stray out of a safe area with a letter in one hand, I was swinging a baseball bat in the other.

One Saturday night we had Mock Court. A student would be brought into the room and questioned, in front of the class and staff, by two other students. The object was to break the defendant's cover. The pair of interrogators could use any and all methods except physical force. We all had a crack at both sides. Each case lasted ten minutes, and the class voted to express their opinion as to who had won the case, prosecutors or defendant.

I had the good fortune to go up against a couple of dim

bulbs, Homer and Raymond by name, and didn't have much trouble. They started off in an eminently predictable manner by asking about my family background, so I claimed I was a bastard, and had absolutely no idea who my father might be. Gordon added to the confusion by roaring, "Bastards all!" every time anyone paused for breath.

Then Ossian and I teamed up to wreak havoc on Student Earl, an obnoxious little bundle of conceit who was Gordon's pet hate. My partner disclaimed any previous legal training, which may or may not have been the truth, but he would have made one hell of a district attorney. All I had to do was add volume to the proceedings. Ossian had Earl on the ropes in five minutes, and then managed to knock two large holes in his cover. We won the case hands down, our only trouble coming from the irrepressible Gordon, who would start a popular demonstration of approval each time we scored a point. I was about to have him thrown out for obstructing justice when our time expired. Upon investigation, we found that certain light-hearted elements had smuggled three cases of beer into the courtroom.

By the time Gordon's turn to be questioned came around, one of his prosecutors had the good sense to charge him with being drunk and disorderly. That passed by acclamation, which disappointed the defendant. He had planned to plead guilty. Since the back benches were resounding to the chorus of a well-known drinking song, the staff, which was doing most of the singing, called off further litigation.

There was still time for Gordon to make an eloquent speech demanding death in the gas chamber for Earl. Most of the jury was out on the lawn playing touch football in the moonlight, but one of those remaining took it upon himself to remind the orator, "Fine idea, but we have no gas chamber."

Gordon's reply was characteristic: "Then build one—that man has got to go!"

Every four days, we had an evening to ourselves. Near the end of our third week, during one of these, Mitch was struggling with his code homework, three others were copying his work as fast as he did it, Gordon and I were playing blackjack for astronomical stakes, and Ossian was deep in a book.

Captain Shine walked in on this group and sprang the news of our first problem. The class would be taken to Baltimore the next morning and turned loose. Each student was expected to spend the day alone, penetrate some factory, plant, shipyard, or similar business engaged in war work, and bring back proof of successful penetration.

Any place in the Baltimore area would do, so long as it was a war plant. Penetrating a brewery or hairpin factory wasn't considered a test of our abilities, such as they were. We would be in civilian clothes, with a maximum of five dollars and no papers. If we got nabbed, we were to talk our way out of it. There was no phone number to call this trip.

I didn't exactly break out in a cold sweat at the thought of someone putting the arm on me, but there was one angle I preferred not to think about. Whoever got caught would probably wind up in the custody of the Baltimore police. I'd heard about those boys; if they put their minds to it, you'd confess to everything from the Lindbergh snatch to the murder of Cock Robin.

We left with Captain Shine's parting words of encouragement.

"Work alone; do the job; I hope to see you all back here by midnight. Good luck."

Gordon provided the epilogue. "And when the man starts with the rubber hose, tell him you're just playing spy. He'll believe you."

In Baltimore our quartet paused long enough for the traditional handclasps, then scattered four ways. Ossian's parting shot summed it up.

"If anything happens to me, get Liebowitz!"

There I was on Charles Street, with instructions to go into the Valley of the Shade and return. If I could do my work and get back to the Mount Royal Hotel—they worked that place to death—by eleven at night, I would return to Area "E" in triumph.

I spent the morning wandering around, mulling over possible targets, and drawing suspicious looks. My ultimate choice was a branch plant of the Revere Copper and Brass Company, which was in a section of South Baltimore honeycombed with alleys. Not that I lacked confidence, but anyone who came after me was in for plenty of exercise.

As I started back downtown, a police squad car drove up and slowed down at the corner where I was standing. There, wedged in the back seat between two plainclothes bruisers, was Student Bob. He looked straight at me, but neither one of us so much as blinked. He didn't; I couldn't. One gone, and he had to go right in front of me.

The minute I walked into my selected target, I wished to God I'd never heard of the place. It was knee-deep in plant police, uniformed security guards, and everyone in the joint wore a large identity badge complete with photograph. The receptionist nailed me before I could pivot and walk right out again, so I asked to see the employment manager with regard to securing a position in the Public Relations Section.

I was given a three-page form to fill out, which I did, hoping all the while that what I said to the man while he interviewed me would approximate what I put on the paper. While waiting to be called, I decided the best "proof of penetration" would be to hook one of the employee badges.

The interview turned out to be a heart-warming affair which made me feel the compleat scoundrel. A kindly, sincere old gentleman looked over the form I had forged, asked me a few additional questions, seemed quite impressed with my mythical employment record, didn't attach any importance to the fact my discharge papers were in a suitcase which had been mischecked and temporarily lost, and ended up offering me a position.

"After what you've been through, Mr. Hawthorne," he said warmly, "I personally would consider it a privilege to have you join our organization."

While I sat there, telling lie after lie, I saw a box on his desk half filled with what I imagined were the badges of former employees. It didn't take long to get one; he got up and went across the room to a filing cabinet, and the moment his back was turned, I made a grab.

I hated the thought of deceiving him any more than necessary, so I asked for a little time to think things over, thanked him profusely, and said I'd call first thing in the morning. On the way out, I stopped in a washroom and took a look at the badge. One glance at the picture and I abandoned plans for a stroll around the Revere Copper and Brass Plant. The rightful owner was a man, but his ancestors came from the Dark Continent.

I left the plant and headed back uptown. It didn't seem wise to wander around the streets with no papers and a "hot" badge, so I took in a double-feature motion picture. Then dinner, which left me with one dollar and two hours to kill. A municipal band concert solved the problem.

Our quartet regrouped at the rendezvous, and we told each other what wonderful agents we were all the way back to the area. Bob wasn't there when we arrived, he'd never shown up at his car for the return trip. I told Captain Shine what I'd seen in the police car, and he hurried off to make a phone call.

Bob was the only student who had run into real trouble; some of the boys hadn't been able to penetrate anything, but they hadn't been picked up. The Captain came back with the welcome news that Bob had been located, he was all right and would be back in the morning. We went to bed on that.

At breakfast Bob came in with the eggs, looking dead-tired and quite chagrined. He'd been nailed on a million-to-one shot, for resembling a racketeer the police had ordered out of town. At the station house, he was able to prove he wasn't the hood, but his lack of identifying papers aroused suspicion, and they'd held him for further investigation. Captain Shine had "sprung" him by calling the O.S.S. contact man in Baltimore.

With all the flock safe in the fold, we had a small critique. Each student got up and told his harrowing tale, then the staff tore his performance to shreds. No one came through unscathed. Gordon was blistered for letting a plant identification photographer take his picture. Ossian got the same treatment for going through an executive's desk while the executive was in the next room. Mitch was straightened out about staying too long once he'd made his penetration. I caught a real blast for coming up with a useless badge.

Actually, Captain Shine and the staff were delighted with our work, but they were too wise to let us know at the time. Whatever else we had, we didn't lack self-confidence.

SEVEN

a Philadelphia story

WE WERE told to prepare for another scheme before most of us had finished fantastic yarns about the deeds allegedly accomplished on our Baltimore junket. Captain Shine went to great lengths to assure us that the first affair had been nursery stuff compared to the upcoming caper. He wouldn't say another thing about it, except that the locale would be Philadelphia. Gordon brightened perceptibly at this news.

"I know what my proof of penetration is going to be this time."

"Oh, what?"

"That statue of William Penn on top of City Hall."

"Certainly a logical enough choice, but I'm not very bright. "Why?"

"It would look great on the front lawn here."

"Colonial, huh?"

"Not exactly. William's holding a rolled manuscript in one hand. Period wise, I'd call it Early American Men's Room."

Our detailed briefing came a day later. The scheme was to last three days and two nights. It called for going to Philly, checking into a hotel, penetrating the specific plant or factory assigned, communicating pertinent information by various methods to one of the instructors who would be along on the problem, then receiving and carrying out further orders from him.

On the surface, it looked easier than Baltimore. We were
to have counterfeit drivers' licenses, false identification papers and credentials, fake letters of reference, calling cards,
even a phone number to call in case things got completely
out of hand.

"What the hell is so tough about this one?" Mitch asked.
"We're loaded with everything we need to get in and out
again, aren't we?"

"Certainly looks that way," I answered. "Seems a piece of
cake compared to Baltimore."

"Captain Shine in no way reminds me of the boy who cried
'Woof!' " said Gordon in a mild voice. "He said it would be
far more difficult. It'll be far more difficult."

"You can bet it will." Ossian sounded quite positive. "We'll
be vulnerable for sixty hours. In Baltimore it didn't take
much more than thirty minutes. Sixty hours. Three days and
two nights. We're likely to need every single thing they give
us and more."

The problem was designed to simulate, so far as was prac-
tical and possible, the conditions under which an agent
would operate in the field. The risk was immeasurably less,
but there was still enough to keep things interesting. Having
a phone number to call was a comfort, but using it would
be an admission of failure.

The school printer was placed at our disposal, with reserva-
tions. My prompt request for an Honorable Discharge certifi-
cate was politely refused, thereby ending dreams of a quick
return to civilian life. All the other things I asked for arrived
the next day. As the clincher for my cover story, I fulfilled a
lifelong ambition and wrote myself several glowing letters
of recommendation.

The night of the final briefing, we each received our individual assignments. Mine was to penetrate a factory which
manufactured circuit breakers and radar equipment. Then
the class was divided into two groups, one for each of the

instructors making the trip. My section drew Charlie, an Area "E" regular. The other half got some unknown wonder straight from the Schools and Training Section in Washington. They also got my deepest sympathy.

Then came the welcome news that we could work together if it proved necessary, and it would be all right to use personal funds if we went through the allotted amount and had time left over. In both instances, Captain Shine warned, "Don't overdo it, gentlemen."

We left the next morning, all except Student Bob. His bad luck held and he came down with such a fierce case of poison ivy the medic wouldn't let him leave the house. None of us envied him then, but there were those in the class who did before the next three days had passed.

We swarmed aboard the proper train in Baltimore and headed for destiny. I was getting used to wandering around in civilian clothes again, and it felt much better with a pocketful of papers. There wasn't a word of truth on all of them combined, I even knocked two years off my age, but it was good to have printed lies backing up the verbal ones. The first problem had tested our nerve more than anything else, this one would find out if we had any ability to go along with the nerve.

If anyone was jittery, it wasn't in evidence on the way up. I had my hands full with Gordon and our ever-present blackjack game. Mitch and Ossian sat across the aisle creating a certain amount of consternation by carrying on a heated discussion in German, which they both spoke fluently. Not content with the harvest of suspicious glares this reaped, they waited until the train was passing the Glenn L. Martin aircraft factories, a huge camouflaged plant area half an hour out of Baltimore. Then Ossian leaned across, and in a stage whisper which rattled the car, asked, "Hans, haff you gott de planz?"

The question was accompanied by a significant glance out

the window. I was busy playing aces back to back at the time, but Gordon had the presence of mind to answer with a guttural "Ja."

I don't precisely know what effect this brief exchange had on the other passengers, but it was enough to make certain of our classmates hurriedly move to other parts of the train.

Our first test in Philadelphia, finding hotel space, was a scheme all by itself. We were under orders to get single rooms, which is what made it tough. Gordon and I bluffed our way into the Bellevue, Mitch and Ossian wound up across the street in the Ritz.

Next step was to call the instructor, tell him I'd arrived intact, where I was staying, and that I was about to proceed as directed. Only it couldn't be done that simply. The conversation was to be conducted as though the wire were tapped. I had to garble the message, the instructor had to ungarble it.

"Hello, Charlie?"

"Speaking. Who's this?"

"Robert Hawthorne."

"Why, hello Bob, how are you?"

"Fine, thanks. I ran into Ezra at the Bellevue last night and he told me you were in town. Thought I'd give you a ring. Wanted to tell you you owe me a dinner."

"Do I?"

"Remember the last time I saw you? We were arguing about who was the first Allied pilot to become an ace in this war. I said it was an Australian named Cobber Cain. Read an article about him in the paper last week. I was right."

"I'll take your word for it. How are chances of getting together with you soon?"

"I've got some work to do, here and there, but I should be able to make it later in the week. Suppose I give you a ring then?"

"Right, Bob, thanks for calling. I'll hear from you soon."

"Fine. So long, Charlie."

The fact I'd called meant I was safe and sound. Mentioning the Bellevue told him where I was bedded down. He knew that my cover name while there was Robert Hawthorne. Bringing the name Cobber into the conversation let him know my student identity. Saying he'd hear from me later was telling me to go ahead as planned.

It was early afternoon, so I wandered over to the circuit breaker plant to look at my target. It was a brick building which covered a city block, with its protection evidently concentrated on the inside. I decided to have a crack at it right away, and walked into the employment office to ask for a job. I filled out the usual forms, and was led off to the inevitable interview. At this point, Dame Fortune stopped smiling and began to laugh out loud.

The interviewer was a lovely young lady, obviously new on the job and ever so eager to do right. Two minutes of small talk proved her to be naïve and extremely impressionable. For lack of an easier method of pursuing my evil designs, I charmed her. She had gone to school in New Orleans, which made that part of my story twice as convincing. The imposing array of self-composed character references and letters of recommendation were the icing on a well-baked cake.

I did change one detail in my cover, telling her I'd been wounded while paratrooping in Sicily in deference to the possibility of her being of Italian descent. Not that it would have mattered if I'd said I'd been hit carrying the flag up San Juan Hill. Her reaction to my "and-then-they-got-me" interlude convinced me that the theme song for this jaunt would be "None but the Purple Heart."

After arranging for me to have a talk with the vice president in charge of something or other the next morning, she asked, "Would you care to have a look around?"

"I'd like that very much. Would it be all right?"

"I'll give you the deluxe guided tour."

For someone so obviously inexperienced at her job, she certainly knew the plant. And practically everyone in it seemed to know her, which helped. When I appeared interested in the protection system, she asked the nearest security guard to explain it to me, after setting his mind at ease with a casual, "Mr. Hawthorne is coming to work for us soon."

She told an eager young man in an assembly room the same thing, and in the process of waxing enthusiastic about the work being done, he mentioned the amount completed to date, and what was hoped for by the end of the year. No one seemed to mind, least of all me. I'd been in the place less than two hours, and my job was three-quarters done.

After a few more questions, I thanked my guiding light for being so helpful, asked her to have lunch with me after my chat with the vice president next day, and went out feeling positively smug. I also shuddered when I thought what a real live agent could have done in that plant.

The Baltimore trip had taught us one thing about all this hoop-la. When we arrived back in Area "E," we'd turn in a complete report on our activities, with all sketches, plans, documents, pictures, badges, and anything else we'd been able to nab while on a penetration mission. If the student agent had uncovered too many loopholes and flaws in a protection setup, the news went to O.S.S. headquarters.

They in turn would send a quiet note to the place in question, informing the powers that their security arrangement wasn't all it should be, and suggesting it might be a good idea for them to tighten things up a bit before an honest-to-God spy came down the road and took the place home with him.

When the clan gathered for dinner that evening, I found the boys had done some penetrating of their own. Gordon and Mitch were in tight at their respective targets, and Ossian had been offered such a good position he swore he was thinking of resigning from O.S.S.

The following day started innocently enough. Charlie, the instructor, called and said he had something for me. This wasn't on the schedule, but we had one of the "hi diddle diddle" phone conversations, and ended up making arrangements for a message pass in the Bellevue lobby.

I found him there at the appointed time, walked up, and said, "Pardon me, have you a match?"

"Yes, here, keep 'em."

"Thanks."

The coded message was somewhere in the match booklet. The pass itself came off without a hitch in spite of the fact that Gordon happened to stroll through the lobby, recognized what was going on, came up behind us, and muttered,

"Don't move, you're both under arrest." Then he walked away laughing quietly while we unfroze and cursed his bones.

I went back to my room, found the message between the halves of the booklet cover which had been slit and repasted, spent fifteen minutes decoding it, and began to wonder if the right people were running this show. Charlie wanted to know where Student Bob was, he'd missed all his checks and calls. Did I know anything about it?

Things had gotten nicely snarled in the higher echelons, and Charlie hadn't heard about Bob's poison ivy. The instructors had come up a day ahead of the class, had no idea the missing student had never so much as left Area "E," and were now on the verge of checking the morgue.

I coded an answer saying Bob was sick but safe at home, put it back in the match folder, called Charlie, made arrangements for another pass, worked it, and dashed off to the circuit breaker company. All this extracurricular mystery had made me late for my appointment with the Vice President in Charge of Hiring Spies.

The young lady in personnel who had set things up looked relieved when I charged into her office bemoaning Philadelphia's taxi shortage. She led me upstairs to the V.P., who just happened to be her father. That explained why the hired hands had fawned all over her the day before. Fortunately for me and the work I hoped to accomplish she said she'd meet us for luncheon, and went back to her own territory. I'd never have gotten anything legitimate done if she stayed around; the O.S.S. was running a poor second. I could penetrate a plant anytime.

Her daddy and I had a famous time together. It didn't take long to find out that football was the love of his life; he was as far gone on it as my Commanding Officer in Louisiana had been on softball. The Army-Navy games were his particular passion, and being a Navy Junior I had seen every one of them in the past twenty years. He was entranced, and I began to have visions of being hired as the Director of Sports. When his daughter came back at noon, I was describing in detail how Slade Cutter won the game for Navy in 1934 with a field goal at Franklin Field. By then I was thinking in terms of nothing less than the Board of Directors.

The old boy insisted on taking us to lunch. I had thoughts of stuffing my craw with expensive delicacies and necking with his lovely heiress between courses. The news that lunch would be in the plant cafeteria left me an embittered man. I could have afforded such a meal myself, but it still meant the heiress.

We entered to the deafening roar of several thousand voices braying "God Bless America" in C, or thereabouts. Of all the days in the week, this one had been chosen for the monthly War Bond Rally. There was a stage in the middle of the floor, and upon it various workers gave their amateurish all. Since

we couldn't eat while the show was in progress, I sat back
and forced myself to watch the "entertainment."

The first act cost me my appetite, the second, a little gem
about Gold Star Mothers, almost cost me my breakfast. I
gritted my teeth and waited for the third. It never came.
What did come on stage was mine host, who got a thunder-
ous reception. He made a brief speech, one of those "Keep-
up-the-good-work" rousers, then suddenly turned and pointed
to me. I never had the slightest chance to duck.

"This gathering is honored by the presence of one of the
boys back from over there, a former captain in the paratroops,
wounded in action and honorably discharged. Let's show him
how we feel about it, and maybe we can get him up here to
say a few words. Fellow workers, meet Captain Robert
Hawthorne of the United States Parachute Infantry!"

That did it. The plant band went into a particularly thrill-
ing rendition of "Dixie," which must have made my New
England ancestors spin in their coffins, and the power of music was never more apparent. The cafeteria mob evidently
had come up North en masse; they were on their feet in an
instant, howling and applauding. I looked wildly at the heiress for help, and that young charmer had tears of pride in
her eyes. I was trapped. There was no choice.

I walked up to the stage, developing a limp en route,
fought back a huge desire to slug the Vice President, waited
for the admiring throng to simmer down, and gave 'em the
business. My previous dramatic experience had been limited
to one performance as The Dormouse in *Alice In Wonder-
land,* as rendered by Miss Mowery's Kindergarten, but it
stood me in good stead.

I thanked the workers on behalf of the Armed Forces for
their valuable contributions to the war effort. I urged them
to buy bonds 'til it hurt. I pleaded for blood-bank donations.
Then I went all out on the subject of writing to the men
overseas, because, "I was in a tough outfit, but I've seen

men walk away from mail call empty-handed with tears in their eyes."

It lasted five minutes, and all the stops came out for a smash ending.

"I've seen it over here, and I've seen it over there. I'm honestly proud, damn proud, of what we're doing in both places!"

I limped off the stage to an ovation. There wasn't a dry eye in the house. The speech made me feel fine, it might even have done some good. I was easily the biggest fraud any of them would ever lay eyes on, but the chances were they'd never know it. I was mobbed going back to the table; the Vice President wrung my right hand, his daughter clung to my left, and I was "in" that circuit breaker plant all the way up to my big ears.

The rest of the day was a sleigh ride. My new employer invited me to dinner on a night when I knew perfectly well I'd be back at "E," but I accepted. Then I went through the mental agony of making another date with his daughter, knowing I wouldn't be around for that either. Kathryn was no ordinary gal, she was a thing of beauty and charm. I had Ossian's idea in mind—send in a letter of resignation and disappear. My respect for the Federal Bureau of Investigation kept me on active duty.

My final act was to tour the plant again, this time with a junior executive who had orders to see I lacked for nothing. When I left, I knew as much about the place as the man who built it. I finally got away by saying it was necessary to start making arrangements to move to Philadelphia. Everyone expected me to start work the following Monday. I wanted to send them a letter saying I'd joined the Office of Strategic Services, an outfit which didn't discriminate against cripples, but Captain Shine forbade that, so Robert Hawthorne just never showed up.

There was a message waiting when I got back to the hotel.

It was from Ossian, addressed to Mitch, Gordon, and myself.

"Dear Spies," it read, "I shall meet you at Bookbinders around midnight."

Gordon arrived while I was dressing. We swapped stories of the day's adventures, and decided both of us had done all the penetrating necessary. Mitch didn't show up, so we left word where we'd be, and departed. As we walked out of the Bellevue, a voice boomed, "Gordon Merrill!"

Which is how people had their cover stories blown to bits. The voice belonged to a young man who proved to be one of Gordon's better friends. There was no use trying to deny it, and no way of shutting him up. He was an actor, in town with a show having a tryout before its New York opening. He talked about having gone to Princeton with Gordon, having appeared in various plays with Gordon, the week ends he'd spent at Gordon's home, Gordon's family, and Gordon's friends.

I stood there and took it all in, while the gentleman being so thoroughly exposed listened helplessly. His trial didn't end with that, though, he had the devil of a time explaining what he was doing. His regular cover wasn't worth six cents, so he had to fabricate one on the spot. I did what I could to help, which wasn't much, since I hadn't the slightest idea what he'd say next. Running into old friends was one of an agent's greatest occupational hazards. We'd been told that often enough. It happened to Gordon while he was with me, and it put him in the soup for fair. He did a masterful job of getting out of it so far as the friend was concerned, but he was a gone goose with me.

After the friend had finally left, Gordon stood there shaking his head amidst the ruins of a cover which had been so good he had dared to use his Christian name as his student name. It was acknowledged to be the most unbreakable cover in our class, and now it lay in little pieces. He took it hard for a few moments, but the reminder I was honor bound to keep any such breaks to myself restored his usual good spirits.

Having nothing better to do until midnight, we went to see the play which had brought Gordon's fellow thespian to town in the first place. Mr. Merrill gained a small measure of revenge by hissing like a ruptured cobra every time the cause of his downfall set foot upon the stage.

We went to Bookbinders at twelve, and found Ossian engrossed in an early-morning paper. As we approached his table he arose, gravely proffered his hand, and said to me, "Congratulations, my boy. I am proud of you."

"Sure you are. Why?"

"Because of this item on page three."

A hero returned from the war, Captain Robert Hawthorne, had made an inspiring speech at a bond rally held at noon yesterday at the so-and-so circuit breaker company's cafeteria. The workers had been deeply impressed. Bond sales had risen sharply. Captain Hawthorne was joining the company's public relations section. The account was most flattering. There were no pictures, for which I thanked God.

Gordon refused to go overboard.

"You're supposed to be a spy, not a bond salesman. Which side are you on, anyway?"

Mitch never did show up, and Ossian abandoned us for a mysterious late date. He had no sooner climbed into a cab, than an all-too-familiar voice boomed, "Gordon!"

"Oh my Christ, not again," he groaned.

But this time we were glad to see his talkative friend, since he was with several young actresses. Gordon went back to being himself, and at his suggestion, I became a talent scout. That proved to be an absolutely smashing idea.

Charlie phoned at an ungodly hour the next morning. He wanted to be sure I had something to do. I assured him I did, and went back to sleep. Then Gordon wandered in, complaining bitterly that Charlie wouldn't stop bothering him. I got up, dressed, and we checked out of the Bellevue in order to duck any further assignments. We spent the rest of the morning doing something we both considered essential to our agent training—watching the City of Philadelphia marble tournament.

We had left word at the Ritz for Ossian and Mitch to meet us for the final luncheon. Only Ossian showed up. We checked Mitch's hotel again, he hadn't been in since noon the previous day. He wasn't the kind who'd vanish without leaving word, and we began to worry about our wandering boy. I called Charlie, and his first words were, "Have you seen Mitch?"

"Not since noon yesterday. What's up?"

"I seem to have lost track of him. Can you get a hold of Ossian and Gordon?"

"Yes."

"As soon as you do, you three better come over here."

We were at the Warwick ten minutes later. Charlie was pacing the floor of his room.

"I just had a call from our Philadelphia contact man. He's located Mitch."

"Is he all right?"

"I'm not sure." He sounded grim. "He was picked up yesterday, by Counter Intelligence men. The local police evidently aren't in on it. Anyway, our man has put the pressure on, and Mitch is to be released into the custody of special agents from Washington."

"When'll they get here?"

"They're here." He reached into a brief case. "You aren't students any more, you're special agents from Washington." He handed us each a badge, a set of identification papers, and tossed me a pair of handcuffs. I glanced at the papers.

"This card has my picture on it. Are these my prints, too?"

"Yes. I had them made before the class left the area. You

three," he paused, "and Mitch. When things go wrong, we let the students take care of each other as much as possible. If you can't handle it, call me immediately." He gave me a slip of paper with an address and room number on it. Gordon and Ossian were already out the door and ringing for the elevator.

In the cab, Gordon mused, "I wonder if this is part of the problem."

"If Charlie isn't genuinely worried," Ossian answered, "he's passing up a great career on the stage."

The address proved to be a large office building. We brushed past a guard, took the elevator to an upper floor, found the numbered room, and walked right in without knocking. What furniture there was had been pushed back to the walls. A beefy young man with an oafish face was lounging in one chair cleaning his fingernails with a tooth-pick. A smaller, wiry type of about thirty-five with an un-pleasant look turned away from the window as we entered.

Mitch was there, too. Sitting in a chair, wrapped in a blanket and wearing handcuffs. A trickle of blood which seemed to come from his left ear had dried on the side of his face. He looked as though the wrath of God had hit him, but he didn't so much as bat an eye when he saw us. His suit, shirt, tie, underwear, socks, and shoes were piled on the desk behind him.

On the way over, we had agreed to let Ossian do the talking.

"I'm Agent Charles, this is Agent Stevens, and Agent Rogers. Here's my identification." His voice was usually soft, but now the words came out as if they were being chipped from flint. "We have orders to pick up a man named Mitchell."

"I'm Berg, this is my partner, Connor." The smaller of the two made no effort to conceal the annoyance in his voice. He jerked his head toward Mitch. "There he is."

Ossian turned and said curtly, "Get dressed."

Mitch stood up, clutching the blanket around him. Ossian looked at the cuffs on his wrists, and said smoothly, "The key, please." Being polite didn't make it sound any less an order.

Connor tossed it to me. I unlocked the cuffs, and Mitch slowly got dressed. It was obviously an effort. When he was ready, we started toward the door. Ossian asked, "Do you want a receipt for him?"

"No, that won't be necessary." Berg sounded anxious to get it over and done with.

In the elevator, Mitch managed a tired grin.

"I might have known it would be you three." We didn't say anything because of the operator.

On the sidewalk, Gordon asked worriedly, "How do you feel?"

"Rotten. They worked on me all yesterday afternoon, most of the night, and again this morning." He was looking up at a church steeple across the street. "So that's where the chimes are."

"Why didn't you call Charlie?"

"They kept hitting me in the face with a wet towel." He felt his ear gingerly. "Made me angry more than it hurt."

Ossian was trying to flag a cab.

"Where'd they nail you?"

"In the lobby of the Ritz." He was disgusted. "Damned if I know what went wrong. Those questions they asked were stupid."

A taxi pulled up, Ossian got in, followed by Mitch. I started to open the front door, but Gordon took my arm, then stuck his head in and said to Ossian, "Take him back to Charlie. We'll join you shortly."

As they drove away, Gordon stood staring up at the building we'd just left.

"I knew Mitch before the war. He couldn't get into the service because of a broken ear drum. His right ear." I could guess what he was thinking.

"Now don't go dramatic on me. We can't start slugging C.I. men just because they roughed up a friend. That's part of their job."

"I don't think they're C.I. men. I've seen Berg around 'Q' Building at least three times, and that big goof Connor looks familiar too. I'll bet an arm they're both in the O.S.S."

I was too surprised to say anything.

"Probably students up here on a problem," he went on. "Another class from another area."

"Suppose we go right back up there and find out."

They were putting on their coats when we came in the second time. Gordon looked at them intently.

"I haven't seen you around 'Q' Building for a while, Berg."

"What?"

"You've got a bad memory for faces," Gordon said pleasantly. "That could cause trouble in your line of work."

"I don't know what you're talking about, Stevens."

"Then let me tell you. You're not C.I., you're O.S.S. You knew Mitchell was too, I don't know how you knew it, but you did. Maybe you saw him around Headquarters or an area. You figured he was up here on a problem, and you picked on him so you could practice interrogation. You didn't even bother to try and catch him in a mistake."

I knew Gordon had to be guessing, but he certainly was convincing. Berg made one last effort to bluff his way out of it, but his voice was nervous this time.

"You've got this all wrong. We're Counter Intelligence agents. The kid didn't say anything about being in the O.S.S., he should have told us instead of giving us a hard time."

"You knew he was O.S.S. Interrogating him is one thing, slapping him around is something else."

"Why don't you guys stop crying and get the hell out of here?" Connor spoke for the first time. "We made a mistake. What do you want us to do, say we're sorry?"

It was over seconds after it began. Gordon threw one

gorgeous right hand which caught Berg square on the nose and sent him sprawling. Connor came at me, grabbing a chair on the way. It was as though Major Fairbairn were standing beside me.

"And if they pick up anything, such as furniture, wait until they lift it to strike you, then move in and go for the belly."

Up went the chair and in went my fist under a cheap belt buckle halfway to my elbow. The chair crashed down behind me. Connor gasped and started to bend double. I put everything I owned behind a clout in the horn which dumped him beside his partner.

They were both finished for the day from the looks of them. Gordon bent over and cleaned out their pockets, humming the Princeton Cannon Song.

"Did you learn that in college?"

"What, the song?"

"No, how to roll your victims."

He tore their identification papers to bits and scattered the pieces out a window. As we walked toward the door, Gordon glanced back at Berg and Connor as they were struggling to their feet.

"Have a nice time counter-intelligencing your way back to Washington. And don't forget to tell the instructor what happened to your papers."

When we arrived at the hotel and told Charlie our story, he shook his head in mock disapproval.

"Not that I blame you, but you should have let us handle it. We don't even know who they are."

"You shouldn't have any trouble finding them," said Gordon airily. "Ask the dispensary to be on the lookout for two guys with no noses."

Mitch was being treated by a local doctor who decided he ought to stay overnight and get some rest. A quick check showed the remainder of the class intact, so we started the return trip. Cars were waiting at the assigned locations in Baltimore, and there was a large supper for us at the area.

Around the table, time was devoted to seeing who could tell the best yarn about Philadelphia. I won hands down with my Bond Rally episode. When certain skeptics said I was lying through my teeth, I pulled out the newspaper clipping, tossed it in front of them, and graciously accepted their apologies.

The staff finished up the evening with a critique of our work. The difference between this and Baltimore was that they admitted we'd all done well. A goodly number of the class had finished their assignments in the first two days, and the instructors had been kept busy handing out more work. In the main this consisted of meeting a student on a street corner and telling him to tail a passing stranger for the next two or three hours. Gordon was horrified.

"Can you imagine doing that in Philadelphia? Thank God we went to the marble tournament."

Mitch arrived back next morning. He looked much better and said the doctor told him that the ear had suffered no permanent damage. Then came an unpleasant surprise in the form of a three-hour written exam covering practically everything we'd been trying to absorb over the past four weeks.

It being the last night we had a farewell party, similar to the fling at Area "S." This time the staff made no effort to conceal the real object. Captain Shine even went so far as to explain things at dinner.

"I shall name a student, and the rest of the class, man by man, will tell precisely and exactly what they think of that student. Not only what, but why. We're not interested in purely personal criticism. There must be valid reasons for your likes and dislikes."

It started quietly enough, but about halfway through on

the first name, the harpoons began to fly. From then on, anyone who thought he'd been going to school with twenty-one ardent admirers soon learned differently.

I was generous with both the rose and the thorn, most of the latter going to Student Homer.

"He's overly cautious and possessed of a superiority complex for reasons which are quite beyond me."

Ossian flayed Homer too.

"He gives every indication of having been brought up by a succession of maiden aunts."

Earl caught it from all sides, Gordon outdoing himself in this particular instance. Mitch and Ossian garnered most of the approval, Gordon and I were highly praised for our abilities and resoundingly damned for our irreverence. When it came time for me to comment on Gordon, I rose and said, "He's too belligerent."

A big, affable moose named Student Raymond, overcome by things in general and rye in particular, burst into tears when he began to talk about me.

"I don't care what the rest of you say, I think Cobber's right. I wish I had his attitude. What's wrong with being devil-may-care in this business? It's better than being too serious. I know, because I'm too serious. That's why I worry. Maybe it makes me overemotional." He collapsed on the couch, sobbing.

Gordon shook his head sadly.

"A fine class leader you've been. The horrible example you set has broken poor old Raymond completely."

"Bats! Poor old Raymond has been sloshing down too much poor Old Overholt."

By the time the twenty-second student had suffered verbal crucifixion, we were all rather well stitched. At Ossian's insistence, we told the staff what we thought of them. The high point of the evening came when Raymond underwent a startling transformation which turned him from a weeping willow into a mighty oak. He allowed as how he now considered himself to be twice the man any of us were or ever would be.

The festivities continued into the smallest hours, Gordon and I being the last survivors. We tottered off to bed swearing eternal friendship and agreeing on one thing above all others: No matter what else happened at an O.S.S. school, you could bet they'd get you plastered the final night.

The morning was death with bird songs. After the usual ashen farewells, we headed back to Washington. Those who cared to made plans to meet after the class dispersed. Gordon and Mitch both showed up as civilians, which was no surprise. Our treasured companion, gallant little Ossian, never did meet us. We knew then he was in the agent business too deeply to risk being seen in public with known O.S.S. personnel.

I phoned Moose to tell him all was well.

"And don't go sending me off to another school right away. I've had enough for a while."

"You won't have to worry about that. Sailing time is near."

EIGHT

bon voyage, indeed it was

THE TEN days which followed may not have shaken the world, but they gave "Q" Building a jolt. Erik, Gordon, and I were all awaiting the same thing—overseas shipment orders. We had nothing to do officially, just check with Headquarters twice a day to see if the first alert notice had arrived.

Packing for what lay ahead was a ritual which brought us to the edge of complete lunacy. No one was going to the same place, no one was taking the same things. Erik and I had three complete sets of gear—personal, Government Issue Military, and O.S.S. Issue, the last being different since he was going to the North African theater of operations and I was headed for the European. Gordon, ticketed for the Middle East, had personal, Government Issue Civilian, and O.S.S.

In spite of Moose's frantic pleadings and enraged screams, three hopelessly intermixed piles began to rise in his office, which was near the supply room. The Sergeant in charge of equipping us developed a nervous tic and the habit of talking to himself. Several other people closely connected with the job of getting us out of the States went him one better and started talking about requesting transfers to another branch.

There was the happy day when we took over the stencil machine and cut our own baggage labels. Having been issued a sizable quantity of equipment for which we could

foresee no earthly use, each of us knocked out a stencil with
a fictitious shipment number under our name. These we stuck
on our extra lockers, which were then carefully packed with
such collectors items as:

"One Whistle, Thunderer."

"Ten pins, tent, shelter half."

"Two poles, tent, shelter half."

"One case, water repellent, food bag."

"Chemical Warfare Accessories and Equipment, Including
Clothing."

"One manual, 'What to Do if the Ship Sinks.'"

"One manual, 'How to Get Along with the French.'"

"One manual, 'How to Get Along with the British.'"

We put the lockers out where the baggage detail would
find them. I never saw mine again. Erik's followed him like
an unrequited love, and finally was delivered to his quarters
in Karachi, India, some eighteen months later. He said the
manual about the British came in very handy.

The morning after the stencils dawned with the telephone
ringing as though its little alloy heart was about to bust. I
pried open one eye and discovered that five people were
sharing the double room Erik and I called home. Gordon—
I knew he'd be there—and four young ladies. The extra one
must have been the chaperone.

The caller was an O.S.S. doctor, reminding me today was
the day we'd sworn to come and have our overseas physicals.

The medics earned their money that morning. They had
to certify we would last for two more weeks. If we fell dead
on the way over, it was their fault. Before things were finished, they would have welcomed the blame.

They asked Gordon to read the eye chart, and he asked
them to turn on the lights. They asked Erik to read the color-
blindness test plates, and he promptly identified everything
as plaid. They asked me to hop ten times on one foot, then
hastily asked me to stop after I toppled over twice in the first

three hops, taking some costly medical equipment with me the second time.

Our combined blood pressures scarcely totaled up to a normal one. The Doc who checked our heart beats and pulses had a hard time finding either, the one who listened to our lungs winced, put aside his stethoscope, tried us again bare-eared, and announced that the sounds reminded him so much of Canadian honking geese that he was homesick for his native Maine.

Someone who should have known better sat us down in three chairs side by side, told us to cross our legs, and gave us a reflex test. He hit Gordon on the knee, missed the mark, and Erik kicked. He hit Erik on the knee, missed again, and shut his eyes to keep from seeing Gordon kick. When he whacked me he was finally on the target, so we all kicked.

I demanded an extensive visual chart test, claiming I had bad vision, only to be squashed by a corporal's, "Your eyes are all right, sir. We counted them, you have two."

The aural perception test was licked before it came near us. Erik said he'd have no part of it until the bees were removed from the room. Gordon politely requested a postponement until the riveting stopped. I took the examination to get another crack at the Corporal. He asked me to repeat what he said.

"One, two."

"Button my shoe."

He gave me a hard look, and went on:

"Protestant."

"Episcopalian."

"What did you say?"

"What did you say?"

"Are you trying to be clever?"

"Are you trying to be clever?"

"Three, four."

"Shut the door."

"What's your name?"

"What's your name, sir?"

"Well, what is your name, sir?"

"Call me Candy Bar, I'm half nuts."

"No wonder they're shipping you over."

"I'll send for you when it's safe."

"Please be serious."

"Please be serious."

"White House."

"They got McKinley."

"You seem to be able to hear very well."

"I beg your pardon?"

"I said you seem to be able to hear very well."

"Beg your pardon?"

"You can hear perfectly!" By this time he was shrieking. Erik walked in and asked me, "What's the matter, that guy deaf?"

Then a complicated printed form. A major told us to "fill it," and we spent the rest of the morning filling things. The result of all this, a foregone conclusion, was that we were found physically fit for service outside the continental limits of the U.S. They underlined the word "physically."

After all this, we trooped over to "Q" Building. On the check list, "Things to Do before Going Overseas," some disciple of Charles Addams had seen to it the final slot would be filled with "Make Your Will."

Headquarters generously provided a mimeographed form with blank spaces strategically placed thereon. The "corpse to be" filled them in, had it notarized, and was then free to croak with a clear conscience, safe in the knowledge that his family would be stuck with all his debts.

We ran into a snag when Gordon tried to leave half his nonexistent estate to "the man who shoots Fulton Lewis, Jr.," and the notary refused to notarize. Moose came in during the proceedings—he was thought of as our keeper, they may have sent for him—and became highly indignant because no one was leaving anything to him. His ruffled feelings were soothed by the sight and sound of Gordon trying to square himself by drawing up another will in which he left half his estate to the notary.

There was a method in his madness, the notary being a thoroughly attractive young lady who proudly owned a fine, firm bosom. She also owned, and was wearing, a black dress cut so low Erik admiringly described it as "an umbilical special."

Every time she bent over to lean on her notary seal stamp, those who cared to look could see clear down to her knees.

I lost track of how many times we revised our wills. When that wore thin, some clever lad came along with the idea we should all make out power of attorney forms. They, too, had to be notarized. When Miss Bordens notarized, we witnessed.

Later in the week Erik's orders arrived. He took it courageously, his only objections being to the sentence which read, "This is a *permanent* change of station."

Everyone within earshot was assured he was planning to return. Carrying his shield or on it, he would be back.

The next day, his sailing orders were canceled. The delay was temporary, but it occasioned considerable celebrating, and even more considerable damage to my sickly bank balance. I was rapidly reaching the point where of necessity I had to go one of two places—over the bounding main, or into bankruptcy.

When it finally came to pass, the Norse God's departure was satisfyingly dramatic. As was sometimes the case in the initial phase of an O.S.S. troop movement, it was about as secret as yesterday's ball game, and almost as well attended.

Erik was the last to board the train. After a brief but heartrending farewell, he swung up onto the car platform as it started to move, waved gallantly, then stalked grandly into a door which some thoughtless porter had just closed.

When last seen, Erik the Great was bleeding freely from the nose.

Gordon felt the kiss of death next. He went fast, and followed what had become the accepted pattern. After the party, we sat up all night trying to inveigle the Statler Hotel laundry into returning, clean, the small mountain of work Gordon had thrown their way at the last minute.

He'd left most of his personal packing until the final two hours, between six and eight in the morning, hoping against hope he'd get all his clothing back. It came up, bit by bit, and we packed it as it arrived. Our actions were hampered by those of my date, a fine girl but low on stamina, who would crawl in among Gordon's shirts and shorts for a quick nap if we left her alone near the luggage for a moment.

Gordon's lady fair was no help either. If he went so much as three feet away, she'd wail, "Dahling, come back, it's our last night!"

To which "dahling" would answer, "Be reasonable. I don't plan to be listed as one of the ten best-dressed men in the resistance movement, but I would like to take enough to keep warm and dry."

"Pack in the morning! I adore you!"

"I adore you, but hark, the glow that through yonder window breaks, it's morning. By Oley Speaks."

"Don't leave me, Gordon!" She was in tears.

One small failing marred this touching scene. Three times running she called him different names. Gordon tried lamely to pass this off by telling me they were various characters he'd played on the stage, but I could see it jarred him when she'd bawl out the wrong handle.

If the pathos of the occasion was wasted on me, the humor wasn't. When Gordon wasn't packing, he was either consoling his about-to-be-bereaved love, or picking up the phone and informing anyone who would listen that if his laundry wasn't in his room in fifteen minutes, he'd come down and run the entire staff through their own mangle. Then he'd glare at me.

"Stop laughing and do something."

"You know the rules. No tickee, no laundlee."

"You go Chinese on me, that's all it needs."

We did get to Headquarters on time, minus half Gordon's clothes and nine-tenths of his natural good humor. The last tenth was sorely tried while the transportation officers rushed around frantically searching for another civilian member of the shipment. After a half an hour of waiting, I asked Gordon, "What's the difficulty?"

"They can't locate that idiot Lawrence."

"Why don't they go off and leave him?"

"They seem to think he's going to be the most terrific agent in the history of civilized warfare. Get him into action and victory is ours. There's just one catch."

"What?"

"He don't wanna go."

It took another thirty minutes to track down Lawrence the Lost and drag him forth. By the time the motor convoy started for the station, Gordon was in rugged shape. He stood upright in the back of the truck as it bounced away, bemoaning the lack of bands, cheering throngs, and flag-waving friends. His last words were, "What a way to go, what a miserable way to go!"

My own days were numbered. I requested and got a weekend leave, which I spent in Annapolis. The family didn't like the idea of my going forth to battle, but they did have faith in my ability to take care of myself, so they devoted themselves to making my last days pleasant.

The only difficulty came in explaining that my duty overseas was confidential in nature, and I'd tell everyone all about it the minute I came back to receive my medals. One of my father's indestructible female friends panicked a cocktail party by collaring me and gushing, "Oh Roger, I hear you're in the Office of Strategic Services. I think it's simply wonderful for you to go overseas and entertain the boys!"

I said I could hardly wait to jump with a reel of film under each arm, and a portable screen between my legs.

Leave was cut short by a telegram from Moose. It came collect, and advised me to hurry back. My father and sister bade me a pair of restrained farewells, after which I eased myself back to Washington and walked into the office asking, "Which way to the boat?"

Considering the length of time I'd had nothing to do but get ready, there seemed to be a disproportionate number of things yet to be done. My shipment was O.S.S. through and through—ten officers, four noncommissioned officers, six male civilians, and four female civilians. Three of the officers and two of the noncoms were authorized to wear civilian clothes. They were "Special Bodies." The rest of us went as plain old "Bodies," and right gladly, too.

As embarkation hour drew nigh, people began to appreciate more and more the difference between playing agent over here and being one over there. Going behind the lines was going to be quite enough, and I'd be happy to wear my uniform, thank you.

It went smoothly. Moose was a tower of strength whenever I faltered. I kept my "good-byes" at a minimum in order to maintain my credit rating, put my various affairs in order, and achieved the penultimate by getting my baggage off on schedule. The crowning glory came when I found our port of embarkation was to be Fort Hamilton, which meant the last nights would be in New York.

On the fateful morn, I left the Statler, called Moose and bequeathed him everything I had been forced to leave behind including the bill, tried without success to think of a clever getaway line, and made it to Headquarters almost on time. A colonel called the roll, we piled into trucks, someone yelled "Let's go" as though there were a choice, and we rolled toward the station. I was glad no one came to see me off.

At Fort Hamilton, I was amazed to find the Transportation Corps handling things with a smoothness I never dreamed that branch of the service could attain. We were processed, billeted, lectured, and turned loose until reveille. The trip to New York, combining taxis and subways, took forty-four minutes and cost thirty-five cents. It was the only bargain I came across in the next fourteen hours.

The following day was spent listening to more lectures, seeing instructional films, which was fine because I caught up on my sleep, learning how to climb down the side of a sinking ship, what to do until the rescue craft arrive—"Yes, Lieutenant, they always come"—what to expect of life on a troop ship (damn little), how to contact the post chaplain, and finally an impassioned plea for us to increase our War Bond allotments. Then they turned us out to graze for the second night, and I didn't waste that one either.

We heard the news at the morning formation.

"The following shipments are alerted as of now: blah blah blah IJ 900 HP blah blah blah."

Our Colonel took the group aside.

"Gentlemen, and ladies, the war is about to take on a far more personal aspect for all of us. I am fairly certain we will not be leaving until tomorrow morning, but we are now under security orders, so the O.S.S. and the U.S. Army would appreciate your cooperation." He paused to let this sink in, then added, "Or in plain English, don't go out under the fence tonight."

We spent the afternoon playing softball; the base running was of the kamikaze variety, but no one achieved that which was sought—entrance to the Fort Hamilton base hospital for an indefinite stay. After the game, word came around we were due to embark at six in the morning. Upon hearing these glad tidings, most of IJ 900 HP adjourned to the Officers Club and got stiff.

After breakfast we had a final baggage check, during which everyone made a determined effort to appear unconcerned. Then a half-mile march from the Fort to a ferry slip, passing numerous citizens who didn't bother to cheer. We boarded an ancient bucket, churned up the river at a smart three knots per, disembarked at another pier, and stood waiting to climb up a gangplank which disappeared into what seemed to be the Empire State Building floating on its side. She was nothing less than the *Mauretania*, converted for troop carrying. Even in her war paint, the lady was a queen.

While we were waiting, a swarm of Red Cross volunteers descended on us and distributed candy bars, doughnuts, milk, and coffee with a lavish hand. After cramming my musette bag, left half-empty in anticipation of just such a happy event, I began tossing doughnuts and containers of milk to a ravenous bunch of G.I.'s standing in an open cargo door near the stern of the ship.

They told me they'd gone aboard the day before to help store baggage. In return for nourishment, they gave me what bits of information they had picked up regarding the voyage. How to get billeted where there was hot fresh water, how to get on the best meal schedule, and how to duck the exercise period.

In the midst of this there was a brief renewal of hostilities with the Transportation Corps. A first lieutenant who held down some terribly vital job in the loading detail took it upon himself to shout, "Hey you, stop throwing things to those men."

"And if I don't what'll you do, have me sent overseas?" This had been the standard threat at Camp Plauche, and he reminded me of everyone I'd had trouble with down there.

"I'll report you if you don't stop throwing things."

My answer was promptly reported to a lieutenant colonel, who reported it to our Colonel, who called for me and said, sternly, "Have you any extra candy bars? I only have two."

Five minutes later we went aboard. I was handed two slips of paper, one telling me where I slept, the other when I ate. My meal ticket wasn't the one the boys in the cargo door had recommended, and I created a mild furor by politely asking for an exchange. When the defender of the Empire got it through his head that I couldn't have cared less about being "most irregular," he made the switch. I had broken a British square.

I wandered aimlessly around the lower decks wondering why they'd bothered to print the signs in English until a kind-hearted steward took me by the hand and led me to my quarters. They were something less than exclusive. I occupied what must have originally been an indoor rugby field with three hundred and twenty-seven other second lieutenants. My bunk was the middle one in a tier of three. The Medical Administration Corps was above me, the Air Corps was beneath me.

We had been ordered to stay put, so I practiced Morse code on my life-preserver light—still two words a minute tops—until the battery expired. Finally my mess ticket number was called. I went to the dining hall and was delighted to find four hundred Army nurses already seated. My friends in the cargo door had steered me right. The male officers were assigned to tables apart from the nurses, but seating tickets were being traded before the second course was served. I could only hope the luck of IJ 900 HP would hold all the way over.

Our heroic little band stuck pretty much together at first, then we loosened up and made friends with a number of deserving shipmates, most of whom seemed to be attractive nurses. One named Carol had a fortunate weakness for paratroopers, her brother being one. He also must have been someone's best friend; during three and a half years in the Army, he had risen to the exalted rank of private first class.

The presence of the O.S.S. shipment which included military personnel, civilians, and women aroused considerable speculation. They asked questions, we answered according to our various cover stories. The salt air and fine weather invigorated me to the point where I changed mine every twelve hours. Carol was enthralled. We sat under a lifeboat to keep from being stepped on and became great friends.

The *Mauretania* was speedy enough to go across without the soul-soothing benefit of convoy protection, so we had a variety of drills each day. Lifeboat, fire, collision, enemy surface attack, enemy air attack; the only difference was that during some you went to your quarters, during others you went to your "Abandon Ship" station. The wise boys soon learned to go to the lavatories and keep the card games intact through all kinds.

I browsed around and discovered that a white handkerchief tied around the right arm gave the wearer complete freedom of movement during all drills. This came in handy, especially during antiaircraft firing practice. The British manned the port batteries, an American ack-ack unit which was making the trip kept its hand in by borrowing the starboard guns. Competition impressed me as being on a rather low level; each side fired twice a day for five days and neither hit a thing.

I stood around with my white arm band and listened to the crew of the *Mauretania* blister her paint with their comments.

"Tyke my word for it, old cock, we'll bloody well get knocked for six if we're ever attacked by anything more than flyin' fish."

Life became dull when the sun went down; strict blackout rules went into effect, and no one was allowed on deck. The officers lounge was the next best thing to the last scrimmage before the big game. Officers and nurses who wanted to be alone didn't have a prayer.

All possible spots were carefully guarded by enlisted men detailed to do just that. They were pictures of frustration— men who had sworn that since Army caste regulations prevented them from competing for any love and delight which might be around, the officers damn well weren't going to have any either.

The efforts of the guards were aided and abetted by the senior officers aboard, male and female. I had done battle with she-dragons protecting their young in my day, but for pure dedication to duty, I had never encountered the likes of ranking officers in the Army Nurse Corps.

Five days after we left New York, two Air Corps pilots put their 20/20 vision to work from opposite sides of the ship and howled "Land!" We were in the Irish Sea. Carol came running over and proudly announced, "I've just seen Ireland. What are you looking at?"

"Wales, I think."

"Oh, where? I've never seen one."

Our port of destination proved to be Liverpool. After a few hours spent running down innocent tugs in the harbor, the *Mauretania* splintered a quarter of a mile of pilings and tied up alongside a dock.

The O.S.S. shipment was not scheduled to leave until the following morning. I thought they might try to sneak us off in the dead of night, but the only person who left that way was one of our corporals. He was given permission to take a stroll on deck after blackout, and promptly managed to wander overboard. Fortunately, he landed in the harbor, and was fished out almost at once. If he had fallen from the deck to the dock, we'd have been minus one on the morning report. He walked off a high-riding lady.

The luck of IJ 900 HP did hold right until the end. Someone was considerate enough to leave Carol's detachment on board until the next morning too, so our two groups got together for a Farewell Ball. Whatever else that hospital unit expected to run into, they were certainly ready to handle snakes.

Next morning I leaned on the rail and waved to Carol as she marched down the gangplank and away to war. Then our Colonel called us to the lounge. He'd received instructions to take us down to London, where we'd be parceled out to the various branches.

After a fond farewell to the *Mauretania*, the O.S.S. contingent swung jauntily down the plank to the strains of "Onward, Christian Soldiers," played by a Salvation Army Band. This occasioned comment among the dockside watchers, who arrived at the logical conclusion that we were a detachment of chaplains.

NINE

RWH vs O.S.S., ETOUSA

I HAD BEEN in the Office of Strategic Services long enough to be fairly certain that no one at our London Headquarters would know we were coming. Several of my companions thought otherwise, and backed up their faith by betting we'd be met at the station.

They paid me after our group had spent a lonely hour huddled together in a corner at Paddington. The Colonel in charge of IJ 900 HP had refused point-blank to ask the military police for assistance or directions. Our travel orders were top secret, and he wasn't about to let just anyone have a look. The Provost Marshal himself was finally unearthed for the occasion, and after an icy exchange of military courtesies our Colonel went off to make a phone call.

He came back shaking his head. We not only were not expected, but now that we had arrived, he'd had the devil of a time talking Headquarters into sending someone down to claim us. They did, though, and a half an hour later we were set upon by representatives of various branches, each there to lay hands on the designated number of bodies. I knew I belonged to Special Operations, so when a harried-looking first lieutenant identified himself as their chief slave trader, I went over and announced; "I'm yours."

"You're mine."

"We mustn't."

I was billeted for the night in the Russell Square Hotel, which seemed partial to U.S. Army officers of company grade and unimportant American civilians. Having received an insignificant amount of English money and orders to report to Headquarters bright and early in the morning, I had an inadequate dinner and went back upstairs to write a few letters.

They all had the same theme: I Have Arrived—Victory Is At Hand—Send Food Parcels. When they were finished, I started to crawl into bed and almost dove under it as the air-raid sirens let loose. It proved to be a false alarm, by which time I was past caring anyway.

Half a dozen of my shipment had also spent the night at the Russell Square, and after breakfast we placed ourselves in the hands of an officer who had visited London in prewar days and "knew his way around." He'd been yammering about it since the day we sailed, and I let myself be conned into going with him. He knew his way around all right, around and around and around.

"Listen, you dope, you don't know where Baker Street is and you don't know where Headquarters is and you don't know where we is."

"I know my way around London."

"The hell you do."

"The hell I don't."

"You don't know where we are right now."

"Oh yes I do."

"No you don't."

"I certainly do."

"Where are we?"

"We're lost!"

This kept up until we flagged down a bus, asked for directions to Baker Street, and wound up being dropped twenty feet from the front door. We made it from there alone, were greeted with a noticeable lack of enthusiasm, and put to work filling out all the blank paper which could be assembled on short notice. I signed three pay vouchers and got paid on two of them, a small oversight which was straightened out later without my having to remind them. We were then asked to report back the next morning, and politely told to go away.

Trying to locate some of my Jedburgh friends seemed to be the best idea, so I managed to get separated from the group. Lieutenant "I Know My Way Around London" was casting his spell over the boys again and getting ready to take them sightseeing, and missing that wasn't going to knock the bottom out of my existence.

I had heard the Grosvenor House Officers Mess was the most likely spot to find those I sought, and five minutes after I walked in there I spotted Big John Gildee, a Jed Captain whom I'd known well back in the Area "F" days. He was Boston Irish through and through, and had been held in awe for his refreshing habit of reporting his superiors to their superiors. I thought he'd be surprised to see me, but he was nothing less than startled.

"Rog, for God's sake, how are you? We heard you were all busted up in a jump at Benning and on your way out with a disability discharge."

This, it developed, was a highly colored and slightly distorted version of the cover story I had used at Area "E." It had been so mangled in the retelling that I had been reduced to the status of a bedridden cripple. I denied this the first ten times I was asked about it, then took to admitting I had been shattered to bits, and the fact I was even on my feet, much less back in uniform and overseas, was a tribute not only to my gallant heart but also my indomitable fighting spirit. The Office of Strategic Services was never a place where truth flourished.

But since this was the first time I had heard of my alleged

misfortune, and since John was genuinely concerned, I told him it was a cover gone wrong and not to be confused with the truth. We had a suitable reunion, during which I filled him in on all the latest news from home, and he delivered an invaluable orientation lecture on the London Headquarters and the inhabitants thereof. Captain Gildee had been around for five months, he was a bright young man, and an observant one in the bargain. I paid attention.

"You'll have to get used to taking orders from civilians, the place is swarming with them."

"Fine. I was just getting used to taking orders from the military. Do they know what they're doing?"

"Most of them, but now and then you'll run into someone whose head is solid biscuit."

"What about the Special Operations desk?"

"Run by a man named Terry. I happen to think he knows his business, but you can find plenty of people who'll argue the point. I can tell you right now your trouble over there will come from the exec, a Colonel Stanford. He was born an idiot and he's been losing ground ever since."

"Have any idea when you'll be going in?"

"Soon, I imagine, some of the Jeds have left already. From what I hear the O.G.'s are almost ready, then the whole damn works. You won't be around long, why not go back and try to see Terry this afternoon?"

"Stop shoving, I've only been in London sixteen hours! You've been here six months. I should think it would embarrass you to land in France and find me waiting."

"Not a bit of it, I'd know I was out of harm's way. The chances of you getting there ahead of me are rather remote. Rushing raw recruits into battle isn't the specialty of the house."

"Raw recruit! I started you and the rest of those National Guard rejects on the way to being guerrilla fighters."

"Which might come in handy if we ever go up against gorillas, but I have my doubts about it helping against the Wehrmacht. We spent our first two months over here being made to forget everything we'd learned at all those alphabet areas."

"That shouldn't have been any trick for you."

"Take Big John's word for it, sonny, it will be to your advantage to see Terry as soon as possible. They'll hand you the 'come-back-tomorrow-morning' routine 'til you're over-age-in-grade."

Gildee obviously knew what he was talking about. I made plans to meet him later in the week—"I'm always at the Astor Club after ten"—and trotted back to Headquarters in search of my new boss. Getting in to see him wasn't difficult, I simply told anyone who asked that I was expected, and by the time I walked into Mr. Terry's office, I had him believing it. He had been a banker in Ohio before the war; I never did find out how he ended up as a branch chief.

He was pleasant enough in the saponaceous way peculiar to the breed until they find out you really need the money. We chatted about Washington, mutual friends, my trip over, and finally got down to cases by the simple procedure of running out of anything else to talk about.

Terry said he was considering me for one of three missions. He hadn't decided which, not that it mattered, because none of them was past the initial planning stage. When the rest of my records—which were then in the process of being lost—arrived, he'd make a definite decision and let me know. In any event, it would be a couple of weeks before anything happened. Until then I was to report once a day, and aside from that, I would be pretty much on my own. Any questions, Lieutenant Hall? Only one.

"When will I be going to the British Parachute School?"

"You seem to know quite a bit about us, Lieutenant. In about a week or ten days. Anything else?"

"No, sir. Thank you."

I did, in fact, know quite a bit about them. Big John had seen to that at the Grosvenor House.

I decided a bit of professional sightseeing was in order, and spent the next six days on the prowl. The O.S.S. was spread all over London, a good idea considering what might land on the roof any time. My own particular home base was located close to the American Embassy, near Hyde Park, which was where all the antiaircraft batteries in the western world seem to be emplaced. This sounded comforting, until I learned that the first objective of every raid was to knock out the Hyde Park batteries. Then I began thinking it would be an excellent idea if we moved to the outskirts of town.

In my wanderings through the various buildings, I discovered the watchword was "security," real or imagined. One pass did you no good outside the quarters occupied by the branch which issued it. They acted as though they were jealous of each other, so I acquired a pocketful of passes and the uncanny knack of pulling out the wrong one every time I was challenged. I seldom managed to get in anywhere really interesting, but it kept me off the streets.

But one afternoon, while I was poking around in the Research and Development Building trying to sneak a look at a new gun which was reputed to shoot a bullet which went a mile and then threw rocks, I was set upon by a full colonel, a booming six footer with an iron-gray crew cut, who gave me the feeling the end of the world would be a relatively quiet affair.

"Lieutenant! Do you belong here? What's your branch? Are you busy?"

"I'm attached to Special Operations, sir. Awaiting assignment. No sir, I'm not busy." I wished to God I had been.

"Can you read a war map?"

"Yes, sir." I was hoping he meant the current war.

"You're attached to me for the rest of the afternoon. Come on."

As we left the building, I stuck a handful of passes under the guard's nose, but he was a dedicated young man who had to see the right one. I was shuffling through my collection when the Colonel turned around impatiently and roared, "Sweet Jesus, play cards on your own time, we're in a hurry!"

At this moment, the guard was looking at my post exchange ration ticket, but the sound of that voice made him lose interest in the proceedings. He threw me a quick salute plus a sympathetic glance, and I went on out.

The Colonel motioned me into a command car which was waiting at the curb; during a ten-minute drive he spoke only once.

"May I see your A.G.O. card, Lieutenant?"

He looked at it carefully, then handed it back.

"How do you do, Lieutenant Hall. I'm Colonel Delano."

I'd heard of him, frequently. A one-man gang who had already parachuted into France twice, and fought his way out both times, once through the Pyrenees and once to a P.T. boat at a channel port. Around the organization, he was known as The Big Hitter.

When we pulled up in front of an impressive building which I didn't recognize as belonging to the O.S.S., Colonel Delano sprang out of the car and through the door in what seemed to be one motion. The two guards must have known him—they did more than salute, they practically fell on their knees. I was swept along in his wake, and we came to rest in an immense antechamber which was remarkably well furnished. The Colonel looked around.

"These boys know how to live." There was a slight note of disapproval in his voice. "I don't imagine you've ever been here before, Lieutenant."

"No, sir. I haven't."

"This is Psychological Warfare Headquarters. There's a time and a place for this business, it can save a lot of lives, but I don't happen to think the channel coast of France is the place and I know damn well this isn't the time. Make the invasion, get a beachhead, start fighting inland, then turn the psychos loose."

That made sense to me, and I had a hard time keeping a straight face when he called them psychos. He went on.

"Most of their brass is here today. They have a map of France which is supposed to be a work of art. I know my way around over there, they want to ask me questions."

He obviously wasn't looking forward to it.

"They're not military men, I mean they don't have military backgrounds. Most of them were professors or researchers, and got direct commissions. They're sincere, and I'm told they work hard. If I can help, I will. It's my duty."

He was interrupted by a sergeant who came in and asked us to follow him into another room, a huge place with one entire wall blanketed by a map which belonged in an art museum. It was a beauty, and must have been done by men who were artists as well as cartographers. The Colonel was impressed.

"Now that, by God, is a map!"

It was under a celluloid overlay, which in turn was covered by a neat collection of signs and symbols. My blood chilled—not one of them looked even vaguely familiar. But Colonel Delano didn't know what they were either.

"Lieutenant, what the hell are those markings?"

"I don't know, sir. I never saw them at Fort Benning."

"Benning? Was General Weems there when you went through?"

"Yes, sir. When I went through Infantry O.C.S. and Parachute School, too."

"Fine man, I was his plebe at the Point. Fine soldier.

They'll have to tell us what that scribbling is, then I guess they'll ask me questions. When I name a place, I'll point it out to you, and you put one of these colored flags in. I'll tell you what color. For Christ's sake don't hurt their precious map. Clear?"

"Yes, sir."

We were admiring the map and trying to figure out the art work on the overlay when a door opened and the Psychological Warfare entourage trooped in. Two captains, four majors, four lieutenant colonels, and a colonel who looked as though he might have been the dean of a small college. Colonel Delano took a deep breath, introduced himself, and brought me into the picture.

"And this is my aide, Lieutenant Hall. He reads maps." No one seemed to care.

Things started with a short talk on the value of Psychological Warfare, which didn't sell me on it by a long shot. Each of the psychos was then moved to rise and add his bit in praise of the branch. This went over so big that various speakers started putting the zing on other branches, with what seemed to be undue emphasis on Special Operations and the Operational Group Command. Colonel Delano's face was getting grimmer by the minute. I figured he wasn't going to take much more.

Then they got tired of knocking everything else in the O.S.S., and a pasty-faced major went up to the map and started explaining the signs and symbols on the overlay.

"Here, around St. Mère Église, we believe the troops to be S.S., mostly of Austrian descent. We know how to handle them. If Supreme Headquarters can be made to see that they must give us enough aircraft, we can saturate this area with the appropriate pamphlets and so weaken the enemy's will to resist that our ground forces should have no trouble occupying the town."

"So they know how to handle the S.S.," Colonel Delano

growled to me. "I'd love to tell them the appropriate use the Germans will make of their precious pamphlets."

A fat lieutenant colonel with a beefy red face and a huge cigar arose and went to the map. He turned out to be twice as objectionable as the rest of them put together, and I stopped worrying about Colonel Delano and began wondering how long I'd be able to keep quiet. Then Tubby began having troubles, he couldn't locate anything he was looking for on the map.

"I doubt if airborne troops could be counted on to handle things here at Deauville, er, Deauville, I can't find Deauville."

"You can't find your head with both hands," muttered Colonel Delano.

"Well, never mind Deauville. Here at Granville—." He used his cigar as a pointer, and it brushed against the celluloid overlay.

It wasn't a big fire if you put it up against something such as the blitz, but it was fast and furious and more than adequate under the circumstances. The map didn't burn, it simply vanished in a sheet of flame. Tubby's hand came out medium well done, no one else was damaged to any extent because we all flew out the door as the room filled with dense smoke. Fire-fighting equipment which was intended for bigger things was brought into play, and everything was under control in less than ten minutes.

"That is the greatest thing I ever expect to see," Colonel Delano said on the way back to Headquarters. "I shall never forget you, Lieutenant. You shared a rare moment in my life. If that's psychological warfare, I pass, it's too much for me."

As the command car pulled up at Baker Street, he thanked me and wished me luck, adding, "I'll probably see you again, Lieutenant Hall. You know, I really should send that poor charred bastard a token of my affection, he kept me out of trouble this afternoon. Yes, I should send him something. Think so?"

"Definitely, sir. Why not send him a pipe?"

London seemed filled with O.S.S. personnel, operational and otherwise, whom I'd met in and around Washington. I took to running around with another Special Operations officer, Captain St. Legere, a tall, handsome article from New Orleans who had come into the organization after winning the Distinguished Service Cross in North Africa. He had been born in France, his one ambition was to get back, and we all figured the day he did all hell was going to break loose in the nursery.

The Saint had been fretting impatiently around London for several months, and being a man who appreciated the finer things, he joined an impressive number of upper-bracket eating and drinking places. One of the best of these, The Centurion, was up the street from the main Headquarters, and usually filled with our people around lunch time.

He and I were in there one day waiting for a friend who had promised to turn up a pair of theater tickets, and The Saint was describing in detail the party he planned to give the day I arrived in Paris.

Our conversation was having tough sledding against the voice of a major who was sitting farther down the bar with a singularly vacant-looking blonde. The Saint glanced his way with such evident distaste that I asked, "Who's your loud fellow member?"

"He's a supply officer, don't know his name. Always in here, and brings a different girl every time. He drinks too much and talks too much."

The Major's voice came through, loud and clear.

"You'll have to go to the club alone, I'll meet you there after dinner. There's an operation going in the end of this week, I have to get it ready."

"You'd better be quiet, Major." The Saint's voice cracked over the bar gabble.

The Major was just sozzled enough to become indignant.

"Now wait a minute, Captain, I didn't say anything—"

"You wait a minute!" St. Legere was off his bar stool and at the Major before I could get a hand up to stop him. "You wait until you get back to your office before you talk about operations going in. Open that big mouth of yours once more and I'll put my fist through it and out the back of your head." He had him by the tie knot and was jamming it up under his chin.

Some of our friends helped me untangle them, and I dragged The Saint out the door, still raging. We walked for fifteen blocks before he cooled off.

"First time I've seen your Gallic temper in action."

"I seldom get angry. You should have let me kill him." He meant it.

"What would that have accomplished?"

"He wouldn't be able to sit in a bar and shoot off his mouth about when an operation's going in."

"I don't think he'll be talking any more, he'll be lucky to get off without courts-martial charges. There were a dozen officers from Headquarters in the room."

"You've got a few things to learn about this place, buster."

"Meaning?"

"There won't be any courts martial. There may be an un-official reprimand, and there's an outside chance he'll be re-assigned to another branch."

"In the O.S.S.?"

I must have looked as incredulous as I sounded. St. Legere smiled for the first time since the hassle started.

"Don't bet against it. Can't you look at him and tell he knows somebody? Whoever got him in and brought him this far will keep right on taking care of him. There are plenty of fat cats in this Headquarters watching over each other, but they're generally smarter and much more careful than their Army brethren."

"I don't know about that, I saw some pretty cozy boys in the Army."

"You'll see cozier ones in the O.S.S. Not that jackass I just bumped heads with, I mean the ones who have a real good deal and know it. Do you like the O.S.S. better than the Army?"

"I'd be out of my mind if I didn't."

"So would the boys in the upper echelons, and I've never met one yet who was dumb. There's nothing they won't do to get up there and stay up there."

"Do you know Colonel Delano?"

"He's operational, that's a very different story. I'm talking about some, not all, of the Headquarters bunch. At that, we're lucky. The ones who do the work do it well enough."

" 'Twas ever thus."

"Stay philosophical and you'll stay out of trouble."

"I'll stay out of trouble! Who crawled that Major, you or me?"

"I did, which is fortunate, because I can get away with it. You couldn't, you'd be out and on your way to a replacement depot by morning. But I won't get away with it for being right, that wouldn't be enough. They'll choose to overlook it because I'm valuable."

"And modest, too."

"It's my saving grace, and one which I doubt you'll imitate, so take my advice and don't try to imitate what I did this afternoon either. Not until you're valuable enough to get away with it."

A few days after the incident at The Centurion, I stopped in at Headquarters to pick up the mail, and found a message from Mr. Terry asking me to report to his office at once. He was mercifully brief about it.

"Well, Lieutenant, I suppose you're pretty bored with London by now?"

"No, sir. I like it fine."

"How about a trip to the British Parachute School?"

"What about it?"

"Would you like to go?" He sounded a bit impatient.

"Like to go? No, not really."

"Too bad, your orders have already been cut. You're leaving Sunday at noon."

"Then I'd better go."

"You'll probably enjoy yourself."

"At a parachute school? Bet me."

T E N

they try to get even for Cornwallis

S.T.S. 51—Secret Training School 51—was a parachutist instruction setup situated on the outskirts of Altringham, a
small town eighty-odd miles northwest of London, chosen
because of its proximity to Ringway, the regular British Airborne School. The instructional branch of the British Intelligence Service ran "51," and O.S.S. "special bodies" took
their chute training in seclusion at this school. The actual
jumps were made at Tatton Park, a network of fields adjacent
to Ringway.

Even the O.S.S. officers and men who were graduates of
the U.S. Army Parachute School at Fort Benning had to take
the course at "51." The great majority of "special-body"
drops were made after dark, and since the British had the
night flying rights over the Continent, the operations were
usually flown in their bombers and the jumps were made British style. This meant going out through a hole in the bottom
of the plane's fuselage. At Benning it was simply a matter
of stepping through a door in the side.

I made the trip to Altringham accompanied by eleven
others, none of whom I had ever seen before. We were met
at the station by "51's" chief instructor, Captain Peter Leghorn, a rather nonchalant gentleman whose black beret in-
dicated previous service in the Tank Corps. He seemed

pleasant enough, but his attitude toward American military personnel in general, and O.S.S. personnel in particular, usually bordered on, "They also serve."

A bus took us through the village and out to the school, a lovely old estate complete with lawns, gardens, a small lake with two swans swimming around looking meaner than hell, even a peahen in the driveway. Leghorn volunteered the information that the school's peacock—"Bloody thing was the pride of the organization"—had departed for bliss eternal a few days previous after colliding head-on with a well-kicked but badly aimed soccer ball.

The Commanding Officer was waiting to greet us on the front steps. He was a gruff old colonel called back to active duty from the retired list, and quite content to leave the actual running of the school up to his chief instructor. After a short speech of welcome, he turned us back over to Leghorn, who saw to it that we were fed a hot supper, shown the way to the nearest pub, and told to be back by midnight.

I accepted his invitation to stay in the officers lounge and learn the intricacies of snooker pool. Talk around the table centered mainly on the week to come. I was amazed by the time involved, or lack of it. My opponent as much as accused me of trying to throw him off his game with a barrage of questions, but I kept right on asking.

"So if training starts tomorrow morning—that's Monday —when's our first jump?"

"Tuesday afternoon. Get your hand off the table."

"We leave Friday night, which means five jumps in four days?"

"Right, two on Friday. Will you concede this shot?"

"Concede your Aunt Minnie, shoot. And if the ones who have never jumped before get through this week alive, are they supposed to be paratroopers?"

"Not by a damn sight. They'll be qualified parachutists. You must keep one foot on the floor at all times."

"Would you be so kind as to keep quiet, sir, while I'm playing, sir?"

I thought of the five back-breaking weeks at Fort Benning, and wondered aloud how anyone could be taught even the most basic fundamentals of parachuting in less than a day.

"Like this next shot I am about to execute," Leghorn assured me, "it can be done. You're standing in the light."

We started our training program with the inevitable lecture telling us what was coming. First on the docket was "ground training," which called for leaping off platforms, dropping from swings, and rolling on mats, all with an eye to reaching the point where we could make a landing and walk away from it. During this session, an old U.S. Airborne battle cry, "Don't forget to tumble!" had one of its frequent rebirths. Leghorn was smitten with it, and in a matter of minutes "51" had adopted a new motto.

Then came an hour in a parachute harness swing, learning what to do between the plane and the ground. Finally, practicing exits, the only thing new to me. The hole wasn't nearly as wide as I thought it should have been, and it got narrower at the bottom, but there still was enough room for a man with a chute on to drop through.

The exit sequence started with sitting sideways on the edge, knees drawn up, one hand grasping the edge behind you, the other back of your heels. On "Action stations" swing your feet into the hole and sit as far out on the edge as you could get; on "Go" give a slight push-off with both hands, straighten your legs, throw back your head, grasp the sides of your trousers, and drop on through.

Conking your head on the opposite side of the hole was known as "ringing the bell." Shoving off too hard was almost certain to make you a ringer, and leaning your head forward to look down—the most natural instinct at that point—was absolutely guaranteed to do it.

Leghorn, who kept insisting, "It's damn well-nigh impossible to crack your noggins if y' do as we tell you," looked relieved when we each had completed five exits through the mock-up fuselage with no bloody noses or split foreheads. When I asked him about several partially obscured dents near the bottom of the hole, he smiled, flaked off a bit of paint, and identified the gouges as teeth marks.

"We usually have to touch it up after each class. Someone forgets and looks down. I'd appreciate your not mentioning it to the others though, bad psychology y'know."

The air brake was next on the schedule. A regulation-size hole had been cut in the second-floor porch. On either side of the hole were iron sawhorse braces, standing about four feet high and supporting a small cable drum. The pipe which went through the middle of the drum had four metal fans attached to one end, each fan a ten-inch square. One end of the cable was fastened to the drum, the other secured to a parachute harness.

A sergeant instructor slipped into the harness and demonstrated the air brake. He sat beside the hole, followed the command sequence, and made his exit. The metal fans slowed the drum as it whirled around, and he landed on the mat twenty feet below as though he'd stepped off a chair. Then the cable was rewound, the harness hauled back up, and the students were given a crack at the brake. After we'd each had a couple of trips, Leghorn called off the proceedings.

"That's all for today chaps, you've done quite well. We'll run through exits and landings again in the morning, and if the weather holds good, we'll jump in the afternoon."

Again I spent the evening being demolished in the billiard room. Between impossible shots Leghorn discussed the theory behind the training methods used at "51."

"It's simply a matter of using psychology because we don't have time to do anything else. There is no alternative. How long were you in training at Benning before your first jump?"

"Three weeks counting 'A' stage. That was physical conditioning."

"We have one day to get students ready for their first jump —one day, mind you—and five days at the most to turn out the finished product. There's no time to teach fine points, there's certainly no time for physical conditioning. Psychology, that's the answer."

"Finished product in five days. It's a wonder some of your products aren't finished in the strictest sense of the word."

"There's one other cornerstone in our system. In nine-tenths of the cases, the student who comes here must be taught enough to make just one operational jump. His airborne career will last only long enough to get him in behind the lines. It's a case of teaching the absolute basics, then getting his mind to the point where he has complete confidence in his ability to make what you Americans persist in calling 'the money jump' successfully."

"Well, if it's a con man they need here, they struck pure gold when they dragged you out of one of those tanks. I wish you luck, and it might come in handy. These boys I'm with didn't wind up in the O.S.S. because of low I.Q.'s. If they figure out what's going on around here, by tomorrow afternoon they'll be as steady as something that's just been led from a burning stable."

"In which case I shall count on you to set a shining example."

"You can count on me giving you a shot in the head with this cue if you don't stop shaking the table!"

Tuesday morning was lovely, and Leghorn ruined more than one appetite at breakfast by cheerfully announcing we'd jump right after lunch. Our first instructional period was exits and landings, then a seminar on how a British chute opens, or "develops." I stifled a yawn and wondered if I still knew how to sleep with my eyes open, one of the few real accomplishments of my college career. Then it dawned on me that their way and the method at Fort Benning were exact opposites, so I sat up and paid attention.

American parachutes came out of their packs after the risers and suspension lines, then cracked open suddenly. The terrific jerk this gave the jumper in mid-air was known as "opening shock." The British packed their chutes so the silk canopy came out first, opened gradually, and pulled the lines and risers out, all with no stunning jolt. It was a bit slower, but infinitely smoother and more pleasant.

After the "development" demonstration, Leghorn said he'd skip any further instruction. Instead we'd go over and watch some of the morning jumps being made at Tatton Park by the regular airborne students from Ringway.

"After all," he said, "you lads have learned all you need to know; wouldn't want you to get stale."

This after less than ten hours of somewhat casual instruction. He noticed my look of amazement and asked, "Any comments, Lieutenant Hall?"

"Only one. You must have lost some close relatives at Bunker Hill."

We arrived at Tatton Park a few moments before the first plane came over. It was an ancient Whittley bomber, ideal for training purposes because of its slow speed. After the pilot throttled down almost to the point of stalling, the first man dropped out. As his chute opened gradually, he swung back underneath it as a pendulum. I was impressed by the absence of anything resembling the vicious shock which characterized all the jumps at Fort Benning, and by the fine display of form. Leghorn paid tribute to that by remarking, "Must have been an instructor."

The next student's exit resembled nothing so much as a would-be suicide who changed his mind too late. Head over heels, arms flailing, legs kicking. To make it a complete atrocity, as the canopy filled out the jumper's legs became entangled in the lines and he started his descent hanging upside down. A loudspeaker started blaring instructions, and the student chutist managed to free himself and straighten things out in a matter of seconds. I nudged the Chief Instructor.

"Better call the roll."

"Why?"

"Somebody must have wandered off and gotten in the wrong line. That last exhibition, he had to be one of ours, I mean yours."

Leghorn, whose psychology treatment had suffered a noticeable setback, kept us at Tatton Park until we'd seen enough proper exits to restore our shaken faith in his oft-repeated assurances. The landings were uniformly and fortunately excellent, no student mind seemed troubled on that score. Not troubled, but certainly preoccupied. As our bus pulled up in front of "51," a large Siamese cat which belonged to one of the cooks strolled out the front door to greet us. Someone who was considered normal asked, "What's that?"

"A Siamese cat."

"Where's the other one?"

After lunch, as we straggled into the hangar at Ringway, one of the school's sergeants confirmed something I had suspected all along: I was to jump first. We drew our chutes, and as I walked over to the dressing racks, I had a vague idea something was missing. After I'd adjusted my harness, climbed into it, and gotten all buckled up, I suddenly realized what was lacking. A reserve chute. Once again Benning and Ringway were at odds, and in this instance I took violent exception to the British scheme of things. When Leghorn came over and asked me to help him harness up some of the other students, I balked for a moment on the grounds it would make me an accessory, then gave him a hand. Some of my classmates were beginning to turn a delicate shade of green at the thought of things to come, and I found myself matching Leghorn, psychologically speaking, phrase for phrase.

My most effective morale booster was, "Look, if I can do it, anyone can do it, and I've done it."

I still felt naked without a reserve chute, and while Leghorn and I were having a last cigarette together, I spoke briefly but with great feeling on a subject near and dear to me at the moment, namely, "Would It Break His Majesty's Government to Spring for Two Parachutes?"

Our Chief Instructor replied, "I'm not the least bit worried."

"Why the hell should you be?"

"Chin up, hearts of oak."

"And heads to match. What a homicidal way to save a buck."

A Ringway instructor came over, introduced himself, and said, "Lieutenant Hall, Captain Leghorn has suggested you test jump for the afternoon drops."

"Well that's big of him."

"Yes, quite. He said you'd done it at Benning, you know the procedure. Our people on the ground check to make sure the altitude and estimated wind velocity are correct before the student class is jumped."

"They'll have slide rules out before I've stopped bouncing."

Again I cornered the redoubtable Leghorn and delivered another harangue. This time the theme was, "If I Am Going to Work Here, I Want More Money." He was mumbling about Lend Lease when as number-one man I climbed into number-one aircraft, "F" for Freddie.

Once we'd gotten underway, my only worry was that Freddie would never get off the ground, much less make it to the drop zone. After a series of shudders and lurches we were airborne. The two jumpmasters began to move around hook-ing people up. One of them leaned over and shouted in my ear, "Test jumping, eh? You must know your business."

"I wrote the book on it." Talking seemed to help, so I yelled across the hole to the student opposite me.

"How do you like the way 'F' for Fragile flaps along?"

"I only hope I fall clear when it crumbles. Don't care if this is my first one, I can hardly wait. Takes more nerve to stay in this flying strawberry crate than it will to go out of it."

I was wondering if this was more of Leghorn's psychology when the senior jumpmaster crawled past and straddled the hole. He looked at me and grinned, listened to the intercom for a moment, then shouted, "Running in!"

I wriggled into position, the red light came on.

"Action stations!"

I swung my legs into the hole, glanced at the tense faces of the students bunched in a line on the opposite side, then looked back at the red light. It flicked off. The jumpmaster, whose eyes never left me since he was taking his cues from the intercom, raised his right hand, and I started the pushout.

"Number one!"

The green light blinked on.

"Go!"

I dropped through, saw the tail of the plane pass overhead, watched my chute stream out and develop, felt the merest suggestion of a tug on my harness, and heard the loudspeaker cut in.

"Good show you, number one."

As I steered my chute around, I found it lacked the maneuverability of its American counterpart because the risers and suspension lines were much more difficult to reach, but I was too delighted by the total lack of the dreaded "opening shock" to be in a critical mood. I also made a mental note to apologize to several persons I had refused point-blank to

believe when they told me that, as often as not, you had
to look up at a British chute to be sure it was open.

My landing was a piece of cake, but I threw in a spectacular
roll for Leghorn's benefit. He came down to see if I was intact, finally admitted under considerable pressure that my
exit had been a thing of beauty, and after I'd balled up my
parachute, we trudged across the field toward the loudspeaker. The test jump was evidently satisfactory, because
the planes circled back over the drop zone, and the rest of
the class came out in slow singles. They all did surprisingly
well.

As we rode back to "51" I was still shaking my head.
Twenty-four hours earlier these same students wouldn't have
been sure of the difference between a parachute and a spin-
naker sail; now they'd made their first and hardest jump in
fine style and were well on their way to being qualified parachutists. It added up to a resounding victory for Leghorn's
methods, and I told him as much.

The rest of the week was charming. We learned something
each day, proved it by making the required jumps, became
quite attached to the habit of having tea in the late afternoon,
and caroused mildly in Altringham during the evenings.
One of our number grew quite fond of a lovely young
W.A.A.F. stationed at Ringway, but their romance withered.
He couldn't stand the strain after learning she was a parachute packer.

The first day's jumps had been singles, then we were taught
how to move a five-man "stick" up the plane and out the hole,
three from one side and two from the other. This was hilari-
ous during dry runs; it was also extremely tricky when played
for keeps.

On our second stick jump, I went as last man, number five.
On the way out, the number-three man froze for a couple of
seconds. That was enough to throw number four off his tim-

ing and make him jittery to boot, so he slowed up too. By the
time I got through the hole, the plane had passed the drop
zone. That wasn't serious, but it meant I'd have to steer myself back over the field. The worst thing in prospect was a
tree landing, which isn't sought after but seldom proves
tragic.

Leghorn was on the mike saying soothing words to numbers three and four, both of whom were still shaky and not
handling their chutes properly. As I wrestled mine back
towards the zone, a gust of wind hit and carried me straight
at the instructors grouped around the loudspeaker. By this
time I was too far down to do any more steering. I had to get
ready for a landing which promised to be what was locally
referred to as a smasher. All I could do was loudly inform
Leghorn and company, "All right boys, break it up."

Leghorn turned as his comrades scattered, saw me swoop-
ing down on him, and calmly announced, "And now we
present Lieutenant Roger Hall."

He held the microphone at arm's length over his head,
pointed it at me, and stepped to one side as I swung past,
missing him by two feet and the mike by half as much. It
was my intention to say, "God save the King!" but all the
audience ever heard was, "God!" The rest was lost with my
breath when I slammed in so hard I shook the ground for
yards around. Leghorn's comforting words as he bent over
me were, "Jump when you're supposed to and you'll land
where you're supposed to."

I still didn't have enough air in me to do justice to the
language the occasion called for, but I did manage to rise up
weakly and try to hit our Chief Instructor.

The last morning at "51" came up cold and foggy, the
Middle England weather getting back to normal after four
lovely days. My classmates were disconsolate; they had to
make five jumps to become qualified parachutists according

to U.S. Army regulations, and even though we'd managed to get in two jumps on Thursday, they only had four.

Leghorn came striding into breakfast grinning and rubbing his hands. He looked at all the mournful faces.

"Cheer up lads, you'll make your jumps. I've been hoping for a patch of fog, now we can use the balloons."

"The what?"

"The balloons." He looked straight at me. "This is one time you all start off even. How about that, Roger?"

"How about lying down while I call a doctor, you must be losing your mind. This weather is enough to make the postman call up and say he is sick."

"Be that as it may, we jump in an hour, so hurry and eat your porridge."

I didn't take him seriously until our bus pulled into Tatton Park, then I saw what he had in mind. We were going to drop through a hole in the bottom of a basket hanging beneath a captive balloon, which was fastened to a winch securely anchored to a huge truck. The fog which had grounded our planes wouldn't have the slightest effect on the balloon. No one mentioned the effect that not being able to see the ground might have on the jumpers.

Our chutes had been trucked over from Ringway. While I was buckling up, Leghorn came over and said, "I told you we'd jump, and I'm a man of my word."

"Either put on a chute or ease up on that 'we' talk. And stop looking so pleased with yourself just because you've found a device certain to destroy the class to a man. Before I go up in that damn thing, I want to file an official complaint."

"Go right ahead."

"Where and to whom?"

"Here and to me."

"Oh, great! Think of it as a doomed hero's last wish."

"My pleasure. Now, what is it?"

"Tell the British War Office that this kind of jazz went out of style right after the First World War."

The truck came over towing the balloon, the big bag was hauled down, four of us and a jumpmaster climbed into the basket, and the command was given.

"Send her up eight and down one."

This proved to mean up eight hundred feet and down one hundred. I asked why we couldn't go up to seven hundred feet and stay there, but no one answered me. Then things got too quiet for our liking, so we hung over the edges of the basket and raised an ungodly din the rest of the way up. The jumpmaster finally ordered us to sit in the four corners and be still. Two students promptly began discussing in loud whispers the feasibility of chucking him over the side, cutting the cable, and hoping for a favoring wind to blow us back across the Atlantic. The other one, sitting next to me, kept leaning forward, peering out the hole into a solid blanket of gray nothingness, and yelling to nobody in particular, "Whatta you doing down there George, shoveling coal?"

By the time we were hooked up and ready, the jumpmaster seemed quite anxious to get us out of his basket. I glanced out the hole and noted that the unseen truck was evidently moving slowly, thereby keeping the cable at an angle and out of the jumper's way. We lined up for slow singles. I went last. What impressed me most was the deathly silence. No roar of plane motors, no whistling wind and creaking metal, no shouts, only a quiet, "Ready, sir? Go."

I fell for what seemed like a long, long time, then heard the soft "swoosh" as the chute canopied out and caught hold. Again it was gradual with no shock at all, I had to look to be sure. Since there was no forward motion or prop blast, balloon jumpers fell between one hundred and fifty and two hundred feet before their chutes developed fully.

The fog made the air heavy and I figured my speed of descent was comparatively slow. I came out of the thickest part of the gray blanket about three hundred feet up, watched the ground for a few seconds, and decided to try for a standing landing. If you misjudged your speed and tried it when coming down too fast, a variety of unpleasant things could happen, ranging from snapped ankles through dislocated knees up to and including a fractured spine.

Because of the high accident rate, it was forbidden procedure at both the U.S. and British Parachute Schools, but it was the airborne equivalent of a hole-in-one, so jumpers kept trying to get away with it. Leghorn must have guessed my intent, because the loudspeaker blared, "None of your tricks, number four. Don't forget to tumble."

Which was all I needed. I spread my feet apart—breaking another iron-clad airborne landing rule—and hit within ten yards of the Chief Instructor. There wasn't much of a jolt, I kept my balance and stayed on my feet. Then, before Leghorn could say a reproving word, I took one step toward him, fell to my knees, and finally collapsed at his feet.

The balloon jump wrapped it up. Late that afternoon we were ready for the trip back to London. "51's" Commanding Officer made one of his infrequent appearances, congratulated us for a job well done, and asked Captain Leghorn for a few words. Which is just what that worthy gave us.

"Gentlemen, thank you for not ruining my reputation in its entirety."

During the first part of the train trip, I listened to the tales of heroism and bravery being told by eleven brand-new parachutists. Each man described his every jump in complete detail. I fancied myself a hardened veteran and somewhat above this kind of chatter, so I fell asleep, but when we arrived in London, I was first in line at the Red Cross Club to have the blue-and-white British Parachute Wings sewed on my right sleeve just under the red-and-blue Special Forces Wings.

ELEVEN

Lafayette, my watch was slow

I REPORTED to Mr. Terry's office first thing in the morning. He greeted me warmly.

"Ah, Roger, welcome back. How was your week?"

It was the first time within memory he'd ever called me anything but Lieutenant Hall.

"Fine. You should have covered my bet. I actually did enjoy myself."

"I thought you would. Sit down, we have a great deal to discuss."

The moment I sat down, he got up and started to pace the floor. A minute or so later, he stopped in front of a large wall map of France.

"How are you at reading maps?"

"Colonel Delano thinks I'm great."

"What?"

"Nothing, sir. I can read maps pretty well."

He looked at some papers on his desk, then back at the map. I began wishing he'd get on with whatever it was.

"You keep yourself pretty much up-to-date on the progress of the invasion?"

"Yes, sir. I follow it as closely as possible."

"Hmm. Suppose you show me on this map." If he didn't know, I might as well tell him.

"American armies are here on the west flank, trying to

break through at St. Lo and seal off the Cotetin Peninsula. They want Cherbourg, it's an all weather port. British and Canadians are here, pinned down on the east flank at Caen. We're inland to about here, roughly."

I accompanied this with appropriate finger tracing and pointing. Mr. Terry smiled.

"Good enough, I suppose you know which divisions are where."

"Those of ours that have been identified. The 82nd is around here, the 101st is in here somewhere, the 1st ought to be here, the 29th, God bless 'em, here, the—."

"That'll do. You're up-to-date, all right. Why the kind words for the 29th, if I may ask?"

"They're from Maryland, so am I."

"I see. Now let's see if I can do as well telling you within much stricter security limits what the situation is with regards to O.S.S. units active as of now."

He paused to light a cigarette, and I got the impression he was figuring out how to say something rather than what to say.

"I hardly need to tell you that all of this is information of the most confidential nature imaginable. Its classification is above and beyond top secret."

That, I found myself thinking, would make a helluva rubber stamp—ABOVE AND BEYOND TOP SECRET.

It wasn't, or he wouldn't be getting ready to tell it to me, but I tried to look the way I thought he wanted me to.

"A few of the Jedburgh teams have gone in, but not many, not yet. We want resistance forces organized ahead of our armies, that's their greatest value. There aren't any in Normandy because there aren't any forests or mountains, no place for them to hide. So until the Allies break out of the beachhead, we'll have to wait. There aren't enough Jeds or O.G.'s to blanket France, we have to pick our spots. Ahead of the armies, depending which way they go."

He hadn't told me anything yet, but it was beginning to sound as though he might.

"We have teams here and here, an O.G. here, other teams here, here—" He went on talking and stabbing his finger into the map. Suddenly he stopped, and asked, "Why the puzzled look?"

"You said a few teams, sir. Seems to me they're all over the place."

"Oh, yes. Perhaps I forgot to mention well over half of them are British, so far, including S.A.S. units. Have you heard about them?"

I certainly had. A fearless bunch of British lunatics who wore red berets and roamed around the French countryside in their armored jeeps raising merry old hell. Anyone on either side who valued his life stayed out of their way whenever possible. They just didn't care.

"You can see we have several teams in Brittany, so have the British. It's good country for resistance groups, plenty of cover. The *maquis* are strong in there, ready and able to give the Germans plenty of trouble when the Allies start up toward Brest. We were going to drop you in there to be a liaison officer between the various units."

"Sounds interesting. When?"

"I said, 'were,' Roger." He sounded slightly reproachful, as though he weren't sure I was paying attention.

"Sorry." He was right, I'd been concentrating on the map and trying to figure the distance between the 82nd Division and Brittany.

"Captain St. Legere's team is here, near Coutance, leading a good *maquis* group. As of yesterday, they need another American officer."

An ice-cold owl flew into my stomach and hooked his claws. It must have showed in my face.

"St. Legere's been wounded, not badly. Ambushed, but

they shot their way out of it. Didn't lose a man. However, he was hit in the leg and can't move around too well. You know him, eh?"

"Yes, sir. One of my closest friends."

"Well, he's all right, but he does want another American officer to pinch hit for a while. I guess the morale of the Frenchmen has something to do with it. He asked for you by name."

"I don't pretend to think I could take that man's place, but if he thinks it'll work, I'll go."

Mr. Terry nodded his head, then picked up a folder from his desk and started leafing through it.

"I might as well be frank with you, Roger. St. Legere obviously thinks you're the man for the job, and I can honestly say I do too. But there are those here in Headquarters who aren't so sure. You have an excellent training record, but no combat experience. You speak French, but not at all well. The British Parachute School people gave you top marks, Captain Leghorn being particularly high on you, but you haven't had any other training over here, and there won't be time to give you any more."

He leaned back in his chair and stared at me. I started to say something but didn't. He went on.

"It's not a question of courage or ability, you have plenty of both. It's your attitude. It shows in your records, training, 201 File. You haven't been here long but we've noticed it. I think you'll get over it quickly in France, some other people don't. Do you know what I mean? Precisely what I mean?"

"No, sir, I don't."

"Then I'll do you a favor and tell you. You're much too impatient with inefficiency, either above or below you, and to be fair about it, with yourself, too. In an organization which makes as many mistakes as this one has, does, and always will, too much obvious impatience will brand you as a maverick. No matter what your capabilities, most people won't think you're worth the trouble."

He stopped and let it sink in. There was no point in arguing with him since he was dead right.

"Now, if I send you in to Captain St. Legere, do you think you can keep your opinions to yourself and do what you're told?"

"Yes, sir."

"Are you quite sure?"

"Yes, sir, quite sure. And I'm even more sure that if I didn't, Captain St. Legere would place-kick my head fifty yards on the fly, bad leg and all."

The Branch Chief sat staring at the map and I realized how tired he looked. Suddenly he slammed his hand down on the desk so hard I started half out of my chair.

"Why the hell should my staff and I question the decision and request of a field commander who knows you twice as well as we do? All right, Lieutenant Hall, that's it. You're under operational security as of right now, twenty-four-hour alert. I'll call our R.A.F. liaison and get an aircraft laid on as soon as possible. Go on over to supply and draw your gear, you'll have a choice of weapons, everything else is ready. Be back here at three for further briefing. Where are you staying?"

"Lincoln House, sir."

"Don't check out, we'll take care of that after you've gone. And don't do anything, I repeat, anything, which will give anyone the slightest notion you're going anywhere. Understand?"

"Yes, sir. Any idea about when—"

"Depends entirely on the R.A.F. and the weather, in that order."

"Yes, sir. Thank you."

"There's a better way to thank me, Roger, and you know what it is. I'll see you at three."

Mr. Terry's phone call reached Supply before I did; a corporal was busy checking the sizes on equipment which had been neatly laid out on a long table. A captain with a friendly smile called to me from the other end of the room.

"Hiya, Lieutenant Hall, I'm Tom Coombs. We'll do our best to send you off in good shape."

"Looks that way, Captain. What can I do to help?"

"Well, how about weapons? You want a .45 or—"

"Or nothing, I want a .45."

He chuckled and slipped one out of a nice, new holster. I hefted it and nodded. Coombs kept up a pleasant line of chatter.

"Tell me, Lieutenant, why does everyone want a .45?"

"Knocks down anyone you hit. I'll take a shoulder holster if you've got one."

"Sure thing. Now, carbine or Thompson submachine gun?"

"Both, thank you."

"Where you headed, Berlin? I guess we can let you have both if you really want 'em."

"I do."

"O.K., but we'll have to pack one in the container. Which do you want on the jump?"

"Tommy gun." If there was going to be trouble then, it figured to be in close. The cold owl came to life in my stomach and flapped its wings at the thought.

"Ammo, you can take this much, we'll pack the rest."

"On top, please."

"That's where it always goes. Now, let's check your clothing and boots."

"Mind if I wear my own boots?"

"Not at all, they in good shape?"

"Yes, just had them resoled."

I found myself hoping everyone else connected with the operation did his job as well as Captain Tom Coombs. When the outfitting was completed, he stuck out his hand.

"Good luck, Lieutenant Hall. Give 'em hell. I'll see you when you get back."

"You can bet you will, Captain Coombs. Thanks."

I went down to the Grosvenor House Mess for lunch, which I ate because the signs on the walls made it clear I'd be shot in the back of the head if I left anything on my tray. Then I went back to my quarters at the Lincoln House. Writing a letter home seemed a good idea until I tried. The result frightened me when I reread it, and there didn't seem to be any percentage in upsetting the family. I decided to tell them after it was over and done with.

I was back in Mr. Terry's office promptly at three; he introduced me to a French army officer.

"Colonel Devereaux, may I present Lieutenant Roger Hall."

We shook hands, he had the grip of a blacksmith. The Colonel seemed about fifty, tall, erect, and good-looking except for the faint trace of coldness in the eyes which I had begun to notice in O.S.S. operational personnel overseas. He spoke English a damn sight better than I did.

"How do you do, Lieutenant. Mr. Terry has asked me to assist with your briefing, since I have recently returned from the area to which you are going. Our discussion need not take long."

He turned and touched the map lightly with a pencil.

"Your Captain St. Legere, his partner Lieutenant Levay, and their radio operator, the estimable Sergeant Ashkanasic, are in here somewhere between Coutance and St. Lo. They head a group of approximately sixty-five *maquisards*, fairly well armed and supplied. The Germans are bringing a panzer division up from the Bordeaux region to reinforce their lines, we have reason to believe they will come in about here. Captain St. Legere and his *maquis* will be asked to make the trip as costly and unpleasant as possible."

He started describing the geography of the area, and

although I was paying close attention, I kept thinking that
seventy men against a panzer division was easily the lous-
iest odds I'd ever heard of, much less been associated
with. Colonel Devereaux's smile was notable for its lack of
warmth.

"Perhaps you are wondering what sixty-five or seventy
men can do against a panzer division? Far, far more than
you would ever dream was possible, Lieutenant. I have seen,
I know. In real *maquis* operations, which these are, in real
maquis country, which this is, well-planned and with a maximum of surprise, forty to fifty dead Germans for every
maquisard casualty is not an unusual price."

It struck me as being highly unusual, but I didn't have the
slightest intention of interrupting.

"Attrition; hit-and-run; surprise, kill, and vanish; never
hold ground, never fight an open battle; attack suddenly,
then every man for himself, *foutez le camp,* which roughly
translates, 'Get the hell out of here.' Unmilitary, unsports-
manlike, but terribly effective. In Brittany with its hills, in
the mountains and forests of the Massif Central, the *maquis*
are unbeatable, literally unbeatable."

I was looking forward to seeing The Saint for a variety
of reasons, not the least of which was the opportunity to
tell him that if hadn't been stupid enough to stick his leg in
front of a bullet, I'd have gone to Brittany, where the *maquis*
were unbeatable, literally unbeatable. The Colonel began
to get down to specifics.

"Our British and American allies are, in most instances,
doing a splendid job of not only arming and supplying the
maquis but also furnishing instruction and leadership. Captain St. Legere, in spite of his proclivity for taking too many
chances, has been doing superb work. He will, of course,
continue to give the orders. You and Lieutenant Levay will
be charged with carrying them out. Levay is a French officer,
and it is essential that a uniformed American officer take

part in the operations. The effect on the *maquisards* is incalculable. That, Lieutenant Hall, is where you come in."

So after ten months of brouhaha, I was going to wind up in France as a morale officer.

"Mr. Terry tells me you are quick-witted and intelligent, which is to your advantage. Also you have no combat experience; I happen to think that is also to your advantage. When the *maquis* and their leaders forget they are guerrillas and try to fight the kind of war American soldiers are used to, the results are almost always tragic. You will learn quickly, or not at all. Now, as to the details of your drop."

He pinned a smaller map over the large one of France on the wall.

"We do not know yet exactly where they will set up to receive you. It will be in this general area. The pilot of your aircraft, a British bomber, will fly to the spot at the appointed time. If the proper recognition signal comes from the ground, you will jump when ordered. Captain St. Legere and his men will be waiting. It's as simple as that."

Colonel Devereaux took down his little map and continued in a matter-of-fact voice.

"You are aware of the risk involved. The German High Command is under orders from Corporal Hitler to execute all parachutists, in or out of uniform. Local commanders react to these instructions in different ways. In most instances, you would be lucky if they did no more than shoot you. The solution is simplicity itself: Do not let them capture you alive. I have nothing more to say, unless you wish to ask any questions."

"No questions, sir, except the ones I intend to ask Captain St. Legere."

For the first time since we'd met, Colonel Devereaux smiled as though he meant it.

"It's no easy thing you're being asked to do, Lieutenant

Hall, considering your lack of training. I admire your attitude."

"I'm glad somebody does."

"Pardon?"

"Nothing, Colonel. Thanks for the help, sir."

"Thank you for the opportunity, Lieutenant. Please be so kind as to give my best to Captain St. Legere, and tell him my only regret is that my regards must come to him through a third person."

"I'll do that, sir."

"Gentlemen."

He bowed stiffly, and strode out of the room. I slumped down in a chair and looked at Mr. Terry.

"Whew! Does that tiger know Colonel Delano?"

"Very well. They're like Flagg and Quirt, at each other's throat all the time, but really the closest of friends."

"I'll be surprised if anything in France scares me more than he did."

"You did all right, and if he hadn't thought so, he wouldn't have waited one second to tell me. He's a dedicated man."

"How long's he been back?"

"He came through our line two nights ago, and was flown here immediately. He's already raising hell about wasting time in London. You won't beat him to France by much."

"Which brings us to something of great interest to me. When?"

"Tonight, if the weather holds and St. Legere says he's ready for you."

The owl got colder and redoubled his activity. At least I wasn't going to have much time to worry. Mr. Terry consulted his watch.

"There'll be an officer assigned to you. He'll help as much as possible between now and take-off time. If there's anyone in particular you'd like for that job, I'll try and get him."

"Just make sure it's someone who can lift me. No, wait a minute, how about Tom Coombs?"

"Why, yes, I think I can get Tom for you."

He made a phone call during which I lit one cigarette and smoked two. The owl was winning.

"Captain Coombs will pick you up at the Lincoln House at six o'clock sharp. You'll drive to an airbase, it's less than an hour from London. If the operation is mounted, you'll get a last-minute briefing, then you're off."

"I sure am, 'way off."

Mr. Terry grinned and shuffled the papers on his desk. Then something made him serious again.

"There's one other detail, Roger. The tablets."

"I've got 'em, vitamins and benzedrine. I can be healthy or get stoned, depending on who's winning."

"No, I mean these tablets."

He had reached into a drawer and taken out a small white box, which he placed before me and opened gingerly. In it were two tablets, each a bit smaller than a dime, one white, the other brown.

"The white one is a powerful sedative, it can be swallowed as is or dissolved in water. Half of it will put you to sleep, all of it will knock you or anyone else out cold."

"Nice. What's the other one, an 'L?' "

"Yes, a lethal tablet. Rubber-coated; swallow it and nothing happens, it'll pass right through your system. Bite it, you're unconscious almost at once and you never awaken. I don't need to tell you what it's for. Keep it handy. Taping it to your person is a good idea. You'll be held strictly accountable for it. Sign here."

He shoved a form across the desk; I signed it and pocketed the small box.

"Now that you've destroyed what little was left of my morale, is there anything else?"

"No, except to say again I wouldn't have picked you for

this job if I weren't certain you can bring it off. Good luck, Roger. Be ready on time."

"If I'm there at all, I'll be on time. Thank you, Mr. Terry, see you when I get back."

He nodded silently, we shook hands, I left Headquarters and went to the Lincoln House. By the time things were squared away, it was five o'clock. I wished it were six.

Captain Tom Coombs drove up in a command car right on schedule. I tossed my musette bag in back and got into the front seat beside him.

"Hiya, Lieutenant, how do you feel?"

"Hello, Captain, how do I look?"

"Fine."

"That's not how I feel."

There wasn't much conversation during the drive, I knew talking wouldn't take my mind off things. I was wearing a trench coat; as we approached the airbase Tom handed me an overseas cap.

"Better put this one on, stick yours in a pocket."

"Why?"

"No parachute insignia; the fewer who know what you are, the better."

We stopped at the gate and showed our credentials, then drove on to a small quonset hut about fifty yards from a group of hangars. Captain Coombs parked so close to the door that one step got me out of the car and inside the building. There were three people in a small, cozy room drinking from steaming china mugs. An R.A.F. officer, an R.A.F. sergeant, and Mr. Terry.

"Hello, Roger."

"Hello, Mr. Terry. You come to see me off?"

"Yes, I did."

Which meant it was on and St. Legere was ready for me. I hoped I was ready for him.

"Squadron Leader Heydenryk, Lieutenant Hall and Captain Coombs."

"How do you do gentlemen, this is Sergeant Dumby, he'll be your despatcher, Lieutenant."

Heydenryk was a giant of a man with a bushy handle-bar mustache and a chestful of ribbons. I figured he knew his business, and Dumby, a hard-looking little guy who chewed gum incessantly, seemed equally capable. The Squadron Leader went on after the introductions.

"Perfect weather, clouds and no moon. Your friends are ready, Lieutenant, they'll be waiting. The Eighth Air Force put on the biggest show to date this afternoon near your area, they plastered the jerries into the ground. Some of our boys are going to work over Cherbourg tonight. We'll tag along with them for a while, then make a beeline for Coutance. When I find the lights, you'll get on with it. Take-off time is 0100 hours. The Sergeant and I will leave you now and see you then. If you want anything, use that telephone. You know where to reach me, Mr. Terry."

It was all quite impersonal, which was just as well. I glanced at my watch, eight-fifteen.

"Sorry about this waiting around," Mr. Terry said in an apologetic tone. "I had hoped to get you out of here sooner, but it can't be helped."

"Gives me time to think about the sins of my misspent youth. What are you doing out here, anyway?"

"I'm your branch chief, remember?"

"Yes, I do, and at the risk of sounding maudlin, thanks for coming. Let's play blackjack, I'd just as soon lose my money as leave it with Coombs. You be banker, Mr. Terry."

Eighteen dollars later, I pushed my winnings across the table and told them, "Better buy a copy of Hoyle's. Keep this for me. We'd best get me dressed and check the equipment."

I stripped, then pulled on long underwear, parachute

pants, and my boots. While I was lacing these, Tom brought over a parachute jacket.

"How does this look to you?"

There was an American flag sewed on the left sleeve at the shoulder, Special Forces and British Parachute wings on the right.

"They shouldn't have any trouble figuring out which side I'm on."

"Want to wear a uniform shirt?"

"No, pack it. How about the insigniae?"

Both Coombs and Mr. Terry laughed at my Latin pronunciation.

"Infantry rifles on one collar tab, second lieutenant's bar on the other, parachute wings over left breast pocket."

"It's going to be an early Christmas when the light hits all that. Good Lord, I just thought of something! Have my weapons ever been fired?"

Captain Coombs walked over and picked them up, one by one.

"Yes, they have, fired and cleaned this afternoon. The .45 and tommy gun are perfect, your carbine is zeroed in for 100 yards."

"God bless somebody. Who did that?"

"Me."

"Tom, you're a gem."

I finished dressing, then walked over to have a look at the four containers which were to be dropped with me.

"What's in what?"

"Ammunition in this one, medical supplies and some rations in this one, plastic explosives in this one, your gear in this one."

"What about detonating caps?"

"In with your stuff."

"Thanks a lot!"

I looked at my watch for the fiftieth time, six minutes past twelve. Further up my left wrist was a strip of adhesive tape. The "L" tablet was handy. Mr. Terry saw the tape, too, and turned away quickly. He was staring at the wall as he spoke.

"How about a drink?"

"Another mug of coffee and one of your goofball pills wouldn't even make me yawn."

"I meant brandy."

"Good idea. I might just as well be drunk as the way I am."

He handed me a silver flask and I took a good, stiff slug. The owl seemed to appreciate it.

The door opened and Sergeant Dumby, bundled up in a heavy flying suit, stuck his head in.

"Fifteen minutes, Lieutenant."

"Thanks, Sergeant."

I pulled a camouflage-color British parachute smock over my head, buckled on my belt, and looked at the chute Coombs was holding.

"What color is it, Tom?"

"Dark blue."

"And the others?"

"Dark red, dark green, and dark brown. Your container's dark blue too."

No one was likely to see them on the way down.

"What do I wear on my head?"

"Rubber jump helmet, unless you want a steel one."

"I'll stick with the soft one."

It didn't seem any time at all before Dumby stuck his head in again.

"All set, Lieutenant?"

"All set, Sergeant."

"This way, sir."

I turned and patted Captain Coombs on the shoulder. It may have been the light, but he looked deathly pale.

"Thanks, Tom."

He didn't say a word.

Mr. Terry's voice was soft. "If St. Legere isn't waiting, get back to our lines."

"If he isn't there, I'm going to hide until you send someone to get me."

I shook hands with both of them and followed Sergeant Dumby to the door, through a pair of blackout curtains, and into total darkness.

A plane was warming up and we walked toward the noise of roaring motors. Dumby said something about the weather being good, but I didn't answer because I wasn't sure how my voice would sound. We walked a long fifty yards, and as I caught sight of the plane's outline, I said under my breath, "God give me strength. I don't want to disappoint anyone, myself included."

I sat alone in the belly of a huge bomber, quietly freezing to death and cursing for not wearing my uniform shirt and three dozen sweaters. I figured we must be over the Channel by now. Someone materialized out of nowhere and handed me a cup of hot chocolate, which helped. As I sipped it I thought, this is ridiculous, just plain ridiculous.

My parachute and all the equipment made even the slightest move a problem. Suddenly there was a flash of light through the cracks in the jump hole, the plane bucked and I heard an explosion. Dumby's head came out of the darkness and peered at me.

"Flak," he said calmly.

"I don't envy you guys," I shouted over the motors.

"What do we do that you don't do and jump out of the plane besides?" It was his longest speech to date.

"Nothing, but you do it all the time." He smiled and disappeared.

Later—I had no idea how much later—he came back again and stood for a moment talking into the intercom. Then he and another man—I guessed he was the one who had brought the hot chocolate—pulled off the cover of the jump hole. I didn't look out, I was in no hurry to see occupied France. The motors cut out, and the plane went into a downward glide.

"Action stations," barked Sergeant Dumby.

I put both hands on the edge of the hole and swung my feet down over the side. I'd checked my static line twenty times; whatever else, I was hooked up.

"Running in!"

If there were red and green lights, I didn't see them, not that it mattered. They were Dumby's worry. His face was an expressionless mask, then he bent over and yelled in my ear, "Beat their brains out, sir! Ready number one, Go!"

All the training paid off, I pushed out and dropped through the hole straight as a pool cue. I felt a gentle tug on the harness straps, and looked up at my chute. Coombs must have been color-blind, it looked red, not blue. I twisted around and saw four other chutes strung out behind me. Then I made myself look at the ground. Two large fires about a hundred yards apart, and a half a dozen blinking lights dead center between them. I decided to aim near there— they were moving, which meant people. The tommy gun was across my chest. I checked the clip, pulled the bolt action back and let it slam forward, then fastened the safety. A roar of motors cut in far to the left. Heydenryk had turned and glided as far away as possible before making any noise. I mentally thanked him for that, and also for putting me right in what I hoped was the reception committee's lap.

I was completely relaxed when I hit the ground because I never saw it. My roll was instinctive and effective, I bounced up and spilled the air out of my chute. When the lines sagged, I unbuckled the harness and let it fall to the ground. Behind me I heard a thud, then another, then two more. The containers were down, and close together. Heydenryk and Dumby were quite a pair. I dropped to one knee and listened.

It seemed entirely still at first, then I heard voices, several of them, jabbering in French. I flipped off the safety catch as they came nearer. There were no lights now, just the two fires.

"Où est vous, mon ami?" Someone was shouting now, slowly. "Où est vous, mon ami?"

If he really was my friend, I might just as well find out.

"Ici. Je suis ici."

"Ah!" He sounded ecstatic about it. "Il est ici!"

I could hear them running toward me. A figure came barreling out of the shadows, then stopped short.

"Lieutenant Hawl?"

"Oui."

"Ah!" He grabbed me in a bear hug, then kissed my cheek. Someone else grabbed my hand, a third shadow began patting me affectionately on the head. They all reeked of wine, but that didn't matter a bit. I finally got loose and put the safety catch back on. This was the right place, and these were the right people. Then I heard a familiar voice.

"Rog, is that you?"

"Over here, Saint."

He came hobbling out of the darkness on a cane. We shook hands, and he threw an arm around my shoulders.

"You all right?"

"Sure, how are you, how's the leg?"

"Getting better. How about the equipment?"

"Four containers, back there somewhere." I pointed.

He spoke quietly to the *maquisards,* and they went rushing off in that direction.

"I've got news that's going to turn your hair white, kid."

"Believe me, old friend, if it's not snow-white right now, it ain't gonna be. What's the news?"

"Brace yourself."

"You sound suspiciously cheerful. Have you managed to get surrounded?"

"Hardly. Two hours ago we were overrun by advance elements of the Second Armored Division. You're behind the lines all right, but they're American lines!"

the saints, Mr. Smith, and SHAEF

THREE DAYS almost to the hour from the morning he had told me I was going to France, Mr. Terry rose behind his desk wearing a rather sheepish look as I marched in and fixed him with a reproving glare.

"What a thing to do!"

"Roger, how are you?" He did seem glad to see me.

"I mean, fun's fun, but behind our own lines. Jesus wept! What a thing to do!"

"What can I tell you?"

"You can start by saying everyone connected with sending me in has been stood against a wall and shot dead."

"It couldn't be helped, I give you my word. There's no one to blame, there was nothing anyone could have done. Bradley's breakthrough came as a complete surprise to everyone here. You know I wouldn't have let you go if I'd even suspected what was happening."

"What time did you get St. Legere's report? He swears it was sent before midnight."

"About four A.M., hours after you heard the news yourself."

"Helluva way to run a message center."

"It takes hours to receive, decode, and get a report into the proper hands."

"I could have been killed a dozen different ways. As it was I damn near died of fright."

"I doubt that. Everyone feels like the devil about it, particularly me, and I don't have to tell you we're delighted you're all right."

"Yes you do! How many other people know about the greatest anticlimax since 'For God, for country, and for Yale?'"

"Very few, very few indeed, and they're under strict orders not to say a word about it. The organization is naturally desirous of keeping your recent, er, operation hushed up."

"I can well understand that. The organization can rest assured it will have my complete cooperation."

"Good. Now, how is Captain St. Legere?"

"That Creole son-of-a-bitch almost laughed himself to death. He and his *maquisards* thought my ill-timed arrival was the funniest thing since the Black Plague swept Germany. The only reason any of them are alive today is because they got me so full of red wine I didn't give a particular damn whether I was in unoccupied France or occupied Little America."

"What did you do for two days?"

"Sat in a farmhouse and watched it rain. St. Legere has real trouble getting around, his leg's in worse shape than he'll admit. You ought to order him back here. Levay can handle the *maquis* now."

"How are Levay and Ashkanasic?"

"I never set eyes on either one of them, they went up into the peninsula to see about joining forces with another group. There's plenty of cleaning up to be done before we'll get Cherbourg."

"Did you have any trouble getting back?"

"None at all. Second Armored Intelligence loaned me a

jeep and driver, he took me to Bradley's headquarters near St. Lo, G-2 there gave me top-priority orders and sent me to the Omaha Beach landing strip, and I came back in a courier plane. Incidentally, I gave my gear to the *maquis.*"

"That's all right. How about some coffee?"

"Fine. Why the big rush to get me back here anyway?"

"Something coming up I think you can do better than anyone else who's currently available."

"That sounds vaguely familiar."

"No, I'll guarantee this one personally." He was smiling now. "Take the weekend off and report back Monday at ten. We'll discuss it then."

Even though things had been screwed up to a fare-thee-well, it didn't seem to be anyone's fault. There had been no harm done, and the chances were the story wouldn't get around. I was prepared to let it go at that, and started to leave. Mr. Terry called me back.

"I did forget one thing, Roger." He held out his hand. "The 'L' tablet, please."

It had already been turned over to an amused though understanding Captain Coombs in the supply office, but the Branch Chief hadn't been notified yet. His eyes opened wide as they followed the line of my finger pointing to the cup in front of him.

"In your coffee. That's what happens when I really get impatient with inefficiency."

Mr. Terry gave me a coolish look when I reappeared in his office at the appointed time.

"Good morning, Roger, how are you and the rest of the Borgias?"

"I'm fine thanks, so's Cesare, but Lucrezia must have eaten something that disagreed with her, she was up—"

"Never mind, I'm sorry I asked."

"How are you feeling, sir?"

"Fine, now. It may or may not interest you to know I am not in the Army because I have a heart murmur. I also have a wife and three lovely children. Please remember that in the future. As for your next assignment, it's a bit out of the ordinary."

He made it sound as though my trip to France had been to get the papers.

"Just between you and me, I don't happen to approve of the plan, but it's not for me to decide. This is it, briefly. Our boys have gotten their hands on seven captured German officers, three lieutenants, three captains, and one major, to be exact. After extensive screening and intensive questioning, it has been ascertained that they are now anti-Nazi, anti-Hitler, and pro-us. They will receive special training, then be dropped in ahead of our forces. Their mission will be to infiltrate German units and send back whatever intelligence they can gather."

He obviously didn't think it would work any more than I did.

"Sweet Saint Sebastian, what loonhead dreamed that one up?"

"Isn't it a beauty? Anyway, they've handed me part of the job, and I need an officer—"

"Cut! If you think I'm going to play around behind the lines with any or all of a bunch of alleged turncoats, thanks a lot but no thanks. Get another boy. I'm brave, not foolish."

He shook his head wearily.

"That's not it. I need an officer to take these seven men through the parachute school."

"S.T.S. 51?"

"Yes, the British have agreed to give them parachute training if we'll provide an escort."

"Mercy God, I can see Leghorn's face when I show up with seven Wehrmacht retreads!"

"Then you'll do it?"

"Yes, indeed I will, gladly."

"Good, now all I have to do is find an interpreter. None of your flock speaks or understands enough English to get along."

"How about Jack Goldberg? He's back from France, I had dinner with him Saturday. He speaks German fluently."

"I know Lieutenant Goldberg well, in fact I submitted his name, but some of the powers-that-be don't think he's a wise choice."

"Why not?"

"Figure it out for yourself."

"Because he's Jewish? Well, for Christ's sake, if these guys really have come over to our side, they must have checked their non-Aryan principles along the way. If they haven't, the hell with 'em, they're not worth the trouble. The whole idea is ridiculous enough without making it restricted in the bargain."

"I feel the same way; maybe I can still get Goldberg for you, no one's had the nerve to give me a final no on it."

"I should hope not. Damndest thing I ever heard of."

"Calm down, Roger, you're getting me to the point where I'm likely to tell somebody off and cause trouble doing it. Let's assume Goldberg's going with you. Here's the rest of the story. The seven students will wear British officers' battle dress but no insignia, and they'll have no papers of any kind. You and Jack will have automatics, I think .32's will do better than .45's because you'll wear them in shoulder holsters under your jackets. It's a purely precautionary measure, but I think you ought to have them."

"If you say so, but if these jokers plan to go bye-bye, they'd be fools if they didn't wait until we dropped them back in the fatherland. The way that Patton's balling across France, we'd better hurry. Who's in charge once I deliver the bodies to Altringham?"

"The British. When the training's completed, you bring them back here."

"When do we leave?"

"Tomorrow morning, I hope. You won't get the full course, two or three jumps at the most. Check with me again this afternoon."

When I came back, Lieutenant Goldberg was waiting in the office with Mr. Terry. Someone had seen the light. Jack was a huge, affable boy from Brooklyn who smiled a great deal and let others do most of the talking. The three of us discussed the trip in detail. It had been planned with the utmost care, and looked simple enough if the students behaved themselves. Then Mr. Terry handed us each an automatic with two extra clips of ammunition and shoulder holster.

"Might just as well put them on, see if they fit, and get used to wearing them under your uniforms."

While we were doing this, a phone rang. The Branch Chief answered it, listened a moment, then said, "Send them in."

A door opened and a civilian entered, followed by what seemed at first glance to be seven British officers who'd forgotten their rank buttons and badges. Jack and I finished strapping on the holsters, slipped the automatics in, buttoned up our jackets, and stared back at the men we were to escort through S.T.S. 51. They were hard-looking articles, and all soldier. Precisely one had a face any softer than an axe blade, and he seemed younger than the others.

The civilian introduced himself as a Mr. Von Sogenstein, then said something in German, and presented the men. As each name was called, its owner stepped forward and gave us a beautiful salute.

"Mathew. Mark. Simon. John. Luke. James. Happy."

The last smiled, he was the young one. Mr. Von Sogenstein told us they knew what was expected of them, and assured us of their complete cooperation. Mr. Terry nodded and motioned to Jack, who proceeded to make a short speech in German. They listened attentively with impassive faces, and at one point I realized every man was looking at my boots. Then the conversation switched back to English, arrangements were made to meet in the morning, they saluted again and left.

Mr. Terry turned to us after they'd gone.

"Well, what do you think?"

"If they want to be parachutists, Leghorn won't have any trouble. They're rough. What did you say to them, Jack?"

Lieutenant Goldberg grinned.

"That you were part Indian and the meanest man in the paratroops. Also the fastest and best shot."

"That ought to keep 'em in line. Mention anything about yourself?"

"Only my name."

Everyone was on time at the station. We climbed aboard the train and settled down in the compartments which had been reserved for us. Our charges were under strict orders to talk to no one under any circumstances; anything in the conversation department was to be handled by Lieutenant Goldberg and/or me. This news had little or no effect, they were a tight-lipped crew, and seemed quite content to spend the trip looking out the windows. Things went so smoothly it was dull.

As we pulled into the station at Manchester, I spotted the redoubtable Captain Leghorn pacing the platform and anxiously peering into the cars. We detrained and I strode over to him.

"Hauptmann Leghorn, ich liebe dich. Dein ist mein herzen sehr." My German was strictly from Lehar.

He closed his eyes and half whispered, "Then it's true, they aren't just trying to drive me mad. You have come back, and brought seven jerries with you. What in the name of God have I ever done to deserve this?"

"Meet the boys, they're a swell bunch of fellows, a million laughs."

Leghorn's face froze as Lieutenant Goldberg called the role:

"Mathew. Mark. Simon. John. Luke. James. Happy."

When it was over and the others had boarded a bus, Leghorn caught my arm as I started after them.

"Too bad Judas couldn't make the trip," he hissed. "It's a bit much, don't you think, naming those thugs after saints? The C.O. happens to be a deeply religious man, he'll go crackers when I hand him the roll. Seeing you again would have been enough of a shock, but saints!"

"I came from a poor family and had to work seven days a week so I missed Sunday school, but I still doubt if there ever was a Saint Happy."

The Chief Instructor continued to sputter indignantly all the way to Altringham. I didn't exactly help, not that I tried. Leghorn sought to pin the blame on someone.

"This whole balmy idea could only spring from a mind as simple as yours," he said testily. "This is your work, isn't it?"

"Not my idea."

"Whose?"

"Churchill's."

His face still wore a look of horrified disbelief when the bus pulled up in front of the main school building. I sprang out and raced into the officers lounge, turned the phonograph on, and hurriedly searched through a pile of records. Moments later, as the music blared through the house, Leghorn's anguished howl rose above it.

"Turn that damned thing off this instant!"

"What's the matter, Captain," I asked innocently. "This used to be your favorite song."

"Off, off, turn it off!"

"It would seem," said Lieutenant Goldberg, "that Captain Leghorn is not too fond of 'When the Saints Go Marching In.'"

The remainder of the week was relatively quiet. The unholy six plus Happy went through their abbreviated course quickly and easily, doing all that was asked of them with an almost frightening competence. It took the C.O. a day to recover from the initial roll call, but thereafter he displayed an active interest in the training, and was much more in evidence than during my previous visit. Jack and I made each of the three jumps with our group; there simply was no fault to be found with anything they did. Leghorn admitted as much.

"They're good, all right, as good as anyone I've ever seen pass through here. The only thing close to a flaw is a tendency to be overeager."

"Why not? They're going home."

The trip back to London went off without a hitch. Mr. Von Sogenstein was waiting for us at the station, I turned the men over to him and they marched away without a word. I had orders to report to Mr. Terry immediately so I thanked Lieutenant Goldberg for having been a tower of strength, and went straight to Headquarters.

The Branch Chief listened attentively as I gave him a rundown on the men individually, interrupting from time to time with specific questions.

"Is there any one of them you'd trust more than the others?"

"Well, not really, but if there had to be a choice, I'd take Happy. He might be conning people with that smile, he seemed more human because of it. Jack said he wasn't a bad guy at all. They played chess every night."

"Interesting. Now, is there any one of them you'd be inclined to distrust more than the others?"

"You're damn right there is. Simon. I wouldn't trust that guy out of my sight. Best student in the class, best jumper too, but he's no more on our side than Goebbels is. Never said anything, of course, but he had a sort of built-in arrogance. Jack and I both think you should get him away from the others, he's a bad influence. Simon will go straight back to his Uncle Adolf, and he might just take some of the boys with him."

Mr. Terry made a few notes, thanked me, and said I'd have

a new assignment within the week. Three days later I received an urgent call to report to his office. When I got there Jack Goldberg was waiting outside in the hall.

"Hi, what's this all about?"

"Dunno, they told me to go on in as soon as you arrived."

Mr. Terry was seated at his desk and a man wearing civilian clothes stood with his back to us, looking out the window.

"Roger, Jack, sorry to make you rush over here, but it suddenly became necessary." The Branch Chief was smiling. "May I present Mr. Smith, although I believe you gentlemen have met." The civilian turned with a faint grin on his face. It was Simon.

"Lieutenant Hall, Lieutenant Goldberg, how nice to meet you again." His English matched the cut of his clothes, and they were Saville Row all the way.

We stood there in stunned silence for a moment, then remembered our manners and stepped forward to shake his hand.

"Forgive my rudeness. How do you do, Mr. Smith."

Jack was more direct.

"Oh brother, did you have me fooled!"

Simon nee Smith laughed softly.

"Thank you, and my compliments to you both for the way you handled our group at S.T.S. 51. You, Lieutenant Goldberg, went a long way toward erasing any last doubts about a non-Aryan being their equal. And you, Lieutenant Hall, were all they expected a part Indian paratrooper to be. Now, if you will excuse me, I must go. Mr. Terry will clear up this mystery for you. Good-bye."

As the door closed behind Mr. Smith, Jack turned to Mr. Terry.

"Sir, is that bundle of guts one of our men?"

"No, he was loaned to us by British Intelligence."

"Those six gunsels would have killed him in a minute if they'd known he was a plant."

"He knew that, but we had to have someone in with them to try and find out if they really have come over to us. Smith's been in on the plan since its inception, but he's too valuable a man to risk on the actual operation. When he goes in, it will be alone as a German civilian."

"Well, if he can't get by in Germany, nobody can," said Jack quietly.

One thing puzzled me.

"How come you told us about it?"

"Smith's been taken off the German officer scheme, as I said, his work there being finished. Now he'll be around London for a few weeks on something else. You two are the only ones likely to recognize and remember him as Simon. His six comrades won't ever seen him again if it's humanly possible to prevent it, and by the time they could get another look at him his appearance will be quite different. If either of you should by chance see him in the future, just remember a brave man's life might well depend on how you react, or rather on how you don't react. No reaction at all is best."

Mr. Terry paused and lit a cigarette. I sat there marveling at the combination of intelligence, iron nerve, and sheer courage which went to make up a man such as Mr. Smith. The Branch Chief continued, but his tone of voice seemed much less serious.

"You two might just as well know the whole story. Mr. Smith told us one of the six remaining Germans was an excellent actor but really a diehard Nazi at heart, so he's been taken off the scheme and put back in a prison camp. Now whom do you think that would be?"

The memory of my most recent effort at character analysis was still embarrassingly green, so I went to the most improbable extreme in an effort to salvage something.

"Happy. Right?"

Lieutenant Goldberg was even more astonished to hear our Branch Chief answer, "Right."

For the next couple of weeks, everyone around Headquarters had much too much to do to listen to my bitching about not having anything to do. General Bradley had his armies sweeping toward Paris, then General Patch brought the Seventh across from North Africa and came charging up out of Southern France. As a result, Jedburghs, Operational Groups, Special Operations Units, and agents were being overrun left, right, and sideways.

The O.S.S., in fortunate anticipation of just such goings on, had attached identification teams forward with both Bradley and Patch. Their job was to identify personnel as they turned up and send them back to London. When this news got around via the inevitable grapevine, a number of our more carefree lodge brothers who figured Paris might be more fun began to devote an appropriate share of their efforts to not being overrun.

Mr. Terry finally got around to sending for me and went right to business.

"What do you think of the British?"

"They're our allies, just like the Goumis."

"You seem to be able to get along with them, so I'm assigning you to temporary duty at SHAEF Forward. We don't have anyone there."

"Hadn't you better send something heavier than a second lieutenant?"

"I never noticed you being awed by rank. We need somebody where the work's done. You'll prepare a daily report on the resistance situation in France, take care of the resistance war map, and act on behalf of O.S.S. interests."

"Which reminds me, when's the O.S.S. going to act on be-

half of my interests and promote me? I've been a second for
fifty years."

"I've already tried, you have to be overseas three months.
How does this SHAEF duty sound to you? There's absolutely nothing operational coming up, our problem seems to
be getting men out, not in."

"It's a cheap way to get to France, but at least I'll know
I'm going behind our lines this time."

The Branch Chief winced.

"You'll be in Ops Sub Section, your co-superior officers
being Major Fish—he's American—and Major Ffoulkes—
he's English. You know the way Eisenhower has organized
SHAEF, each American officer has an English counterpart
with the same rank and authority. Only in this case, Ffoulkes
runs the show, he has Fish completely under his thumb. Consequently, the O.S.S. is beginning to get shoved around, it
isn't serious yet but it could be soon. Which is why we want
a man over there. Fish isn't ours, incidentally."

He tilted back in his chair and stared at the ceiling before
continuing.

"You may as well know what you're going up against.
Major Ffoulkes doesn't like Americans. He's nice enough to
the ones who outrank him, but to all others he's about as unpleasant as a human being can get. A hundred years ago he
would have had to fight a duel every day. He's lasted this
long at SHAEF because a British brigadier has him under
his wing. We'll back you up if you get in any real trouble,
but for God's sake try not to."

Two days later I flew across the Channel, landed near
Deauville, and reported to the tent city which was Supreme
Headquarters Allied Expeditionary Forces, Forward. Major
Fish, who reminded me of a jittery Guy Kibbee, shook my
hand warmly.

"Hello, Lieutenant Hall, I'm very glad you're here."

After giving a notably vague description of what my duties were to be, he said in a resigned tone of voice, "Now, I'd better introduce you to Major Ffoulkes."

Who was anything but a fearsome sight, being scrawny with a turtlelike face, horn-rimmed glasses, and a razor cut for a mouth. He acknowledged my salute with an impatient nod, and got right down to being friendly.

"You're late, Hall, we expected you this morning."

I looked at my watch, twenty minutes after twelve. If he ever got ahead, there'd be no catching him.

"It's Lieutenant Hall, sir. The plane landed less than half an hour ago."

"Then you have the Eighth Air Force to thank."

"No, sir, the Royal Air Force."

"Really?" I could have skated on the ice. "Now that you are here, do you know what your duties are?"

"Yes, sir."

His frosty eyes flicked a surprised look at Major Fish.

"Oh? Suppose you tell me."

I did, adding a large chunk of what Terry had told me to Fish's brief effort, and throwing in enough of my own to make the whole thing sound impressive, especially the part about watching over the O.S.S. interests. Ffoulkes was glaring long before I finished. He didn't like the idea of losing the chance to start me off his way, so he came in from a different angle.

"All right, I'll expect you to be at work one half-hour after lunch. And since this headquarters is in a rear zone, you will wear regular shoes, not those boots. That's all."

I had him dead to rights there.

"Major Ffoulkes, I am a qualified parachutist, and as such, authorized by U.S. Army Regulations to wear parachute boots and bloused pants with any uniform up to and including Class A."

That was the beginning of the Thirty Days War. It ended

in a draw, and there were no casualties except poor old Major
Fish, who spent a month on the brink of a nervous collapse.
I didn't lack for allies; virtually every American below the
grade of major knew and loathed Ffoulkes. I prepared my
daily report on the resistance situation and kept the war map
up to date, doing both jobs carefully and well. There was a
twofold reason: I knew it would cost me my head if I made
a mistake, but what was more important, a surprising number of the Americans involved were friends of mine. As for
looking after the interests of the O.S.S., when news of what
the boys had done and were doing began to circulate, the
value of the organization became apparent.

SHAEF Forward moved to Versailles, and I found myself
guiltily hoping Mr. Terry would see fit to let my temporary
duty stretch out until New Year's anyway. Christmas in Paris
had a powerful appeal, and the constant running battle with
Ffoulkes kept things from getting dull.

But Paris had a powerful appeal for others, too. I was
playing with my war map one afternoon when a voice behind me said, "First Lieutenant Hall?"

I turned and came to attention in front of a tall, good-
looking American major with a wide smile and blond hair.

"Afraid not, sir, Second Lieutenant Hall."

"Not any more, your promotion orders are in London. I
would have brought them but you'll be there soon enough.
I'm Major Blackfield." His smile grew even wider. "Your replacement."

I had visited the O.S.S. Headquarters in Paris often enough
to know an ungodly number of field-grade officers were
swarming in from London—several made it all the way from
Washington—as fast as they or their friends could invent
assignments. The Major had probably looked over a table
of organization and found me perched at SHAEF Forward
on temporary duty. By noon the next day I was back in London.

Mr. Terry shook my right hand and shoved some papers in my left.

"Congratulations, on the promotion and the job you did at SHAEF. Nice to see you again, the train leaves for Altringham at three."

"Huh?"

"Detached service at S.T.S. 51, they need instructors badly. Stripped practically clean for replacements to the British First Airborne. Leghorn asked for you."

I knew the Red Devils had been badly mauled at Arnhem, the big war map at SHAEF was right next to mine.

"At least I won't have to worry about anyone coming up and snaffling this job away from me."

The Branch Chief smiled. "No, you won't. They're borrowing you for a month to six weeks. When you come back, I may have a nice Christmas surprise package waiting."

THIRTEEN

headquarters: seldom have so many done so much and accomplished less.

BECAUSE of the necessity of clearing one class out before the next came in, my work at S.T.S. 51 was done on a five-day basis, Monday through Friday. I was there five weeks, and spent each of the week ends in London. Which was all right with me, the Jedburghs were back and the town was rocking.

The great majority of them had gone on their operations late in June and July, expecting to be in the field until the next spring. The rapid advance of the Allied forces, especially through France, put almost all of them back in London by the middle of September with less than twenty per cent casualties (original estimates had been for more than forty per cent). The O.G.'s were back too, and Headquarters was going out of its collective mind trying to figure out how to handle the unexpected deluge of operational personnel.

That took a bit of time, and the resourceful Jeds put it to the best possible use by staking a claim on the West End of London. The Astor Club was their principal watering hole; they liked it and it loved them since they were always colorful and usually solvent. I ran with the pack every time I came to town.

There was the memorable night of the dance contest, when two Jeds—both captains, both giants, and both happy as a box of birds—began a mild argument as to their relative ability to do the Charleston. Since neither had any apparent inclination toward quietude, everyone else in the Astor was more or less forced to take notice. None of the girls —every Jed seemed to have at least one looker—would partner either of the disputants, who seemed to be walking in shaved ice and wearing parachute boots besides.

So they danced together and took turns leading. The sight of those two waltzing bears hopping solemnly around in each other's arms sent everybody up the wall in hysterics, everybody, that is, except a British colonel who should have known better but evidently didn't. He took it upon himself to tell them to stop. What they told him was obscene, although they did add "sir."

"Gentlemen," he said in a voice which left no doubt that he thought they were everything but, "if you do not stop at once, I shall report this to your Commanding Officer."

"Go right ahead," was their joyous answer. "He's playing the drums!"

Then the London brass, who had been devoting a large proportion of their time to setting up and staffing the virtually useless Paris Headquarters, got around to settling the operational personnel problem. The prevailing opinion, bolstered by Washington, was that things in Europe would be wrapped up by Christmas, so the Jedburghs and most of the O.G.'s were given two choices: assignment to the China-Burma-India Theater, or a replacement depot. This didn't set at all well with the boys.

There was a considerable amount of friction between the men who went behind the lines and the men behind desks. Most of it was attributable to the fact that a large majority of the administrative officers and branch chiefs had received direct commissions in the early days of the O.S.S., whereas the field men, many of them combat veterans, had come up through the Army.

There had been an abortive attempt to militarize the higher echelons by bringing in West Pointers, but they tried to run things strictly along the lines of the Army staff system, and that never came close to working. The men in the field were often at fault because they didn't know the whole picture and blamed Headquarters for any and all shortcomings, a number of which were the direct result of policy decisions made at Supreme Headquarters.

But the friction did exist, and when the C.B.I. or replacement depot deal came up on a take-it-or-leave-it basis, the operational personnel let out a wrathful roar of indignation which echoed all the way back to "Q" Building. Another directive was hurriedly sent which said all men who volunteered for the C.B.I. would go there by way of the States, with a thirty-day leave en route.

I was one of the few who turned down this offer, being currently occupied at Altringham, and having been told again by Mr. Terry that something was afoot which would mean a "Christmas surprise" if I chose to stay in the European Theater. He made it sound interesting, so I decided to stick around.

The weeks I spent instructing at S.T.S. 51 went along in a familiar groove until Leghorn figured there should be a suitable reward for my faithful service and badgered the Commandant of the British Parachute School at Ringway into letting me take the hitherto sacrosanct Advanced Airborne Course. Everyone made it sound as though this were a distinction generally reserved for those of royal blood. Before it was over, I was willing to bet someone was out to overthrow the monarchy.

After ricocheting through assorted delights which included an intentional tree landing and a delayed opening free fall, I was subjected to "la specialité de la maison," the water jump. Putting my rubber suit on backwards may have been, as the Chief Instructor swore it was, an honest mistake, but that hardly helped matters. I might just as well have jumped into the frigid lake in track shorts. Three seconds after I slipped out of my harness and plummeted into the water from fifteen feet up instead of the recommended five, I was a bright blue and so was the air around me. And when I bobbed to the surface, the first thing I saw was a speedboat bearing down on me with my British buddy standing on the bow, boathook poised in hand, looking for all the world like Captain Ahab complete with harpoon. There was no way to knock him into the drink and I could only hope that if he did hit me, it would be in a vital spot. I managed to fend him off somehow and inflate my own little rubber boat, but the next time he came by I was too numb to even answer his friendly, "You don't seem to be catching anything, care for a tow?"

I reported back to London and found Mr. Terry had taken a few days' vacation. There was nothing to do but wait until he returned. All the Jeds and most of the O.G.'s had left for the States, and the night life wasn't the same without them. I was moping around the Grosvenor House before dinner one evening when a familiar voice shook the walls.

"Would you like to join me, Lieutenant Hall?"

Colonel Delano was wearing his ribbons, five rows of them, and looked even more impressive this time. He was in a jovial mood, and after a few drinks, insisted on taking me to dinner at Claridge's, the ultimate in English hash houses. A haughty maître d' unbent practically to the point of crawling as he led us to a fine table. The Colonel was obviously well known in these parts. After a sumptuous meal, he swizzled the unlighted end of his cigar around in a brandy snifter. I was fairly glonked by then, and did the same. From the next puff on, opium was for the poor people.

My companion leaned back and gave me a quizzical smile.

"How are you getting along these days, Lieutenant?"

"Pretty well, sir, considering the fact I haven't contributed a thing to the war effort."

"A rather harsh self-indictment. I saw Captain St. Legere on my way out of France, and he told me what happened. Certainly not your fault."

"No, sir, but it still added up to my not doing anything."

"Do you blame the O.S.S. for that?"

"No, I don't. It couldn't be helped."

"I'm glad you understand that. We're in a vast and often chaotic organization of more than twelve thousand persons. It's a wonder there aren't more mistakes."

He paused reflectively, cupping the brandy snifter in his huge hands.

"What do you think is the mission, the job of the O.S.S.?"

"Well, tying the resistance effort of the occupied countries to the military effort of the Allied powers." I'd read that somewhere and managed to quote it verbatim.

"Good enough, but that's only half the story—the resistance half, as it were. Collecting and analyzing strategic information, that's the other half. All those scholars and experts back in Washington, they do a job too. Did it ever occur to you it might be possible to find out more about a railroad line between Paris and Le Havre by consulting available French records and the files of the Baldwin Locomotive Company than by dropping a paratrooper in to look at it?"

"No, sir, but it does make sense."

"Sure it does. The wonder is that Bill Donovan was ever able to get this outfit going in the first place. Do you know how much trouble he had back in the beginning?"

"I've heard the Army and Navy didn't go for the idea."

"They actively opposed it, and the F.B.I. was worse than either of them. Donovan never would have brought it off if he hadn't been such a close friend of Roosevelt's. The chiefs of Army and Navy Intelligence finally came around, but J.

Edgar Hoover sulked and wouldn't even attend the meetings. They gave him the Western Hemisphere, but he wanted more. Can you imagine such a thing?"

"They tell me General MacArthur feels the same way about us."

"Quite true, unfortunately. The Regular Army doesn't seem to place any faith in an American espionage system. The High Command over here was dead set against it until the President put his foot down. They would have much preferred to use the British."

He motioned to the waiter, and after the brandy had been poured went on.

"I'll tell you one thing about the British: Donovan wouldn't have had a chance without their help. Britain, Germany, all the European countries have maintained some form of espionage system for centuries. And I'll tell you something else, I don't think the British would have given him their help if they hadn't figured it was a fair trade for a direct line to Roosevelt's ear. They didn't object to us playing their game during the war, but they didn't like the idea of our being twenty miles away on the Continent afterwards."

He signaled the waiter again, this time for the check. It seemed a good idea, I was fading fast, but the Colonel decided a nightcap was in order.

"I think I'll have another brandy. Care to join me? Good, waiter, two more brandies. Where were we?"

"On the Continent, I think."

"Really? How odd. Anyway, I like to remember among other things that the O.S.S. is the last refuge of men and women who want to do something but don't fit the regulations. You know Virginia Hall?"

"She's my cousin."

"The hell you say! The one with the wooden leg?"

"Naw, must be another Virginia Hall."

"Maybe I'd better finish your brandy."

"I'll manage somehow, sir. Tell me about the wooden-legged virgin."

"Give me that brandy. Miss Virginia Hall parachuted into France with a wooden leg, did a superb job as an agent, and is now trying to talk Headquarters out of awarding her the Distinguished Service Cross. Ed Lord jumped in, he's fifty years old. Henry Lassucq is sixty-three, for Christ's sake!"

"I'm just a boy, maybe that's my trouble."

"Not at the moment it's not."

The Colonel paid the check and we made our way to a cab. It seemed easier for him than it was for me.

"Where do you live, Lieutenant?"

"11 Murray Avenue, Annapolis, Maryland. Drop in any time."

"Thanks. I meant in London."

"Oh. Lincoln House, Knightsbridge. Terribly posh joint, I hope I make it."

"I'll see you do."

The ride home revived me slightly and I was able to listen as Colonel Delano mused, "The Office of Strategic Services, they ought to call it 'Donovan's Baby.' You know what he told me?"

"Nope."

"That when all is said and done, his prayer is that the credit will go to those who volunteered for duty with the express understanding they would never get any credit."

"I think I know what he means, but I won't be sure 'til tomorrow. Here we are, home is the hunter, home from the hills, and the sailor home from the sea. And Roger is home from Claridge's, bless his little heart. Good night, sir, thank you for one helluva fine evening."

He guided me to the door and we shook hands.

"I enjoyed it too, and if I don't see you again, good luck in Norway."

"Good luck to you, Colonel Delano. What? Norway!"

He grinned back at me from halfway down the steps. "There's only one Norway. Good night, Lieutenant Hall."

Mr. Terry made it official the next afternoon; I was now assigned to the Norwegian Section of the Scandinavian Branch. It was the first time I'd heard of either the branch or the section, so the Chief filled me in.

"They're in charge of planning and putting into action the resistance program which has been outlined and approved for Norway by the combined Chiefs of Staff. It may not ever become necessary, but in the event it should, it'll be handled by the Norwegian Section."

"Are they going to use the Norwegian O.G.'s?"

"One of them. The other is ticketed for the C.B.I. They both came back from France pretty much intact."

"That sounds as though I'm going to wind up back in the O.G.'s after all."

"Eventually, but first you're to help with the planning of a suitable mission and the mounting of the operation. When that's done, you'll join the group and go along."

"I seem to be in this thing up to my neck."

"You are, and so are the British."

He smiled as I groaned at the thought of SHAEF and Major Ffoulkes.

"To be more exact, your job will be to maintain liaison between us and British Intelligence. Directing and supplying Norwegian resistance is supposed to be a joint U.S.-Anglo affair, but you may as well know right from the start that the British are determined to keep Norway in their sphere of influence. You should have a lovely time."

"This whole deal has an all-too-familiar ring about it. The only thing you've left out is the line about my being the best available man. Will there really be an operation into Norway?"

"I can't promise that, but if there is, you'll go on it."

"Fair enough. Who's in command of the section?"

"Commander Vettelson, U.S. Navy, direct commission. Born and raised in the old country, a well-known yachtsman, personal friend of King Haakon. He's a delightful old gentleman, and a millionaire besides."

"The last part did it, we'll be buddies. Anyone else over there I ought to know about?"

"Yes, Major Axel, the exec. He's hard working and conscientious, he's also ambitious and inclined to be overly cautious. The British have been wrapping him around their little fingers. One reason we're putting you in as a liaison is to keep them from stealing our pants. Think you can do it?"

"You're talking to the man who survived Ffoulkes once and Leghorn twice. Perfidious Albion isn't likely to top their efforts anytime soon, although I must admit I do like Peter Leghorn. Yes, I think I can do it."

"So do I. You were picked for this job because I think you're the best avail—."

"Don't say it!"

I reported to the Norwegian Section of the Scandinavian Branch the next morning, and found the Commander and Major Axel to be precisely as Mr. Terry had described them. Then I went across the hall and met the British Intelligence officers assigned to the Norwegian Office. They were quite something, a pair of Scots in suitable regalia—Major Peter Douglas of the Seaforth Highlanders and Captain Hamish Frazier-Campbell of the Argyle and Sutherland Highlanders. Both wounded in the North African Campaign, decorated, and placed on limited duty.

A colonel ostensibly ran their part of the show, but I never did meet him because he was never around. The staff referred to him as "Otis the Unseen." Peter planned missions which sent men and supplies to Norwegian resistance groups, Hamish was in charge of getting them ready to go. Whatever those two thought should be done usually got done, one way or another. In less than a week I knew the Commander and Major Axel were hopelessly overmatched.

The two Scots couldn't have been more friendly toward me. They knew precisely why I was dogging their heels and acted accordingly. They couldn't have cared less about my keeping Major Axel up to date on what they were doing, and whenever there was a conflict of interests, either Hamish or Peter would pull a look of injured innocence and say, "But Major, we were under the impression that particular problem was ours."

It always worked. The Major wouldn't have offended those he called "our British comrades" for anything in this world or the next. I only wished he could have been around when Hamish would start his daily tirade about, "Another memo from that silly ass, Axel. More of his damned, stupid rot. Have another cup of Bovril, Rog."

As Christmas drew nigh, things got more and more confused in the Norwegian Section, and it became apparent that if something drastic wasn't done quickly, the Operational Group would never knock off any Germans unless they took to gunning prisoners of war. General Donovan finally bypassed London Headquarters and sent a trouble shooter from Washington to straighten things out. He couldn't have picked a better man for my money—Captain Ralph "Moose" Elsmo.

His arrival was a complete surprise, and seeing him again was a Christmas present if ever I got one. When the news reached the Norwegian Operational Group's area, all the officers drew their back pay and descended on London. Their impact was almost as staggering as the Jeds' return from France. Moose strove mightily to strike a happy medium between the business at hand and the pleasure underfoot. It would have killed a lesser man, but he managed somehow to do his work during the day and still run the best of his companions into the ground at night.

His first order of official business was to put Major Douglas and Captain Frazier-Campbell in their places, politely but firmly. Then Major William Colby, a former Jed and one of the top guerrilla leaders developed by the O.S.S., was put in command of the O.G. First Lieutenant Tom Sather was his executive officer, First Lieutenants Blain Jones and Glenn "Rocky" Farnsworth were his junior officers. I was to join them when planning was completed to the point of a definite target being selected. The reformed group was christened "Norso," after Norwegian Special Operations, and sent to Scotland for ski and mountain training.

Moose locked horns with Major Axel from the start, and even tangled with the Commander, although they were close friends. He didn't have the rank, but he did have an order from the General, and it gave him authority to do everything short of negotiating a separate peace with the Finns. Then someone turned up Colonel Hans Skabo, a Norwegian-American who was Regular Army, and he was put in charge of the Norso Group Operation. Two days after he walked in, we were a going concern.

Captain Elsmo arranged his letters of commendation in a pile an inch thick and went up to Scotland for a week of skiing with his old comrades. I divided my time between watching Hamish and Peter outfit the secret agents being sent into Norway by the British, and doing whatever I could to help Colonel Skabo and my commander-to-be, Bill Colby. He was a slight, wiry graduate of Princeton who had come out of France with an enviable reputation. His officers and men swore by him right down the line. We got along famously right off the bat.

Moose came back in time to spend a classic New Year's Eve at the Astor Club. Next morning I was awakened by strange noises coming from his room, which was next to mine. I stumbled in there, and found the Captain running around with a .32 automatic in hand.

"Hold it, I have some aspirin."

"Out of my way, I'm on a mouse hunt."

"You got a license?"

"Little bastard's been scratching around all morning, keeping me awake. I plugged up the hole, he's in here somewhere. There! Move your foot!"

A grey blur streaked across the room and suddenly stopped still in full view. Moose took careful aim.

"I'm betting on the mouse. The way you're shaking you couldn't hit the floor with a handful of buckshot."

"Quiet, you'll frighten him. I'll blow his head off. Just tell me one thing."

"What?"

"Which one is he?"

I disarmed my vengeful friend, unplugged the mouse hole, and the three of us went back to bed.

Two days later Moose boarded a plane for Washington. He was carrying *A London Tourist's Guide* to read on the trip.

The Norso Group didn't come into being any too soon; our troops on the Continent started to roll again, and Headquarters realized that if there was to be an operation into Norway, it had better get cracking. The Russian penetration in the extreme northern tip had been stalled. The Germans started to pull some of their best units out of there, send them down to southern Norway, then try to shuttle them into the battle for Europe. The British Navy made the trip by sea virtual suicide, so most of the troops moved overland on the Nordland Railway.

The men involved were crack soldiers, most of them from mountain regiments, and veterans of a long, rugged campaign against the Russians. They'd never been defeated in the true sense of the word; their retreats had been more in the nature of strategic withdrawals under orders. There was a considerable body of opinion at SHAEF which thought that with troops of such high caliber, the Nazi High Command might hole up in the Norwegian mountains and make a last stand. Whether or not this came to pass, it was a known fact they were bringing strong reinforcements down from the north and sending them into Europe.

To impede these troop movements, Operation Rype was set up. Colonel Skabo and I had become good friends, and he told me the details in his bluff, hearty manner.

"The Norso Group will parachute in and cut the Nordland Railway wherever possible by blowing up bridges, tunnels, and track. They'll also do whatever damage they can to German lines of communication."

I whistled as he thumped the large map of Norway which hung behind his desk.

"That is going to be one bitch of a job."

"It most certainly will. Skiing instead of marching, fighting winter guerrilla warfare in hell's own conditions against terrific odds. I wish I could go."

Of all the times I'd heard that said around Headquarters, this was the first time I believed it.

The British took a dim view of Operation Rype; they didn't like the idea of American troops going into Norway and made no bones about it. The Norwegian Army High Command in England was something less than enthusiastic, too. They were afraid the appearance of Allied soldiers would touch off a resistance uprising which could not be supported.

Consequently, a great many obstacles had to be overcome before Operation Rype was mounted. Colonel Skabo gave as good as he got from the British and Norwegians, with an assist from Colonel Bohland, a stiff-backed West Pointer who was looking for more action and hooked up with Norso. Between them they whipped Rype into shape, and by the middle of February, things had reached the point where I was ordered to join the Norso Group in Scotland.

FOURTEEN

Scotland and Norway

TOM SATHER met me at the Perth railway station and we jeeped over to Area "P," the O.S.S. name for Dalnaglar Castle, located in the foothills of the Grampian Mountains about ten miles from the town of Blairgowrie. It had been selected because the surrounding countryside was thought to be excellent for ski training and mountain climbing, but whoever chose that particular piece of real estate didn't know a thing about castles. Dalnaglar may have been quite the spot when Bonnie Prince Charlie roamed the land, but by the time the Norso Group arrived, it looked as though it had fallen flat and then been reassembled by a gang of lunatic apprentice stone masons.

When I showed up there was still some snow around, but not enough for any more ski training, which was unfortunate, since Major Colby was able to throw his physical conditioning program into high gear. Long runs and endless hikes under full pack were the order of the day every day, and I had a rough time of it the first week. The rest of our time was devoted to firing various weapons and blowing up everything in sight on demolitions problems, with Rocky Farnsworth proving time and again he was a master of the latter art.

There were a few attempts at organized games, but after the first rugby match compiled an all-too-impressive list of walking wounded, the Major ordered us to stick to volley ball. Since there was only one ball and a single net, play was limited to less than half the group at a time. This bored the other half, so a soccer game was arranged, with strict rules as to body contact.

The only suitable terrain was about a mile from the castle; we all trooped down there one afternoon, a field was lined out, goals were erected after Rocky had blown post holes in the frozen ground, sides were chosen, everybody made bets, and the game started. Play was hardly the caliber you'd find at the Olympics, but the men loved it. Just as things were getting exciting, a flock of sheep came down an adjoining hillside and wandered into the fray. While we were trying to shoo them off the field, a gorgeous collie dog came bouncing into view, and right behind him the angriest shepherd in kingdom come.

He looked old enough to have fought with Robert the Bruce, and he hadn't lost his touch. His initial explosion dealt with the damage we had done to the pasture. Then he roared, "Yer fearin m'sheep, and them aboot to be lambin'! Git off m'land!"

The Norso Group, every man a veteran of guerrilla warfare in France, shifted their feet uneasily and looked to the officers for guidance. Rocky whispered to me, "We got him outnumbered fifty to one, if you don't count the dog."

"I don't think it's going to be enough."

It wasn't, not by a long shot. The ancient Scot suddenly lifted his staff shoulder high, shouted to the collie, and the two of them charged straight at us. Our retreat was rapid and disorderly, but highly effective. A minute later the old boy had his pasture all to himself. He also had the only soccer ball.

Major Colby, who had been watching the game through binoculars from the front lawn of the castle, met us as we trudged back.

"My heroes! Turn in your gear, I'll send him and his dog to Norway."

The men trained hard six days a week, and were in corking good shape because of it. Those who wanted to could go into Blairgowrie on Saturday nights. The local populace wasn't hostile but they weren't exactly friendly. The pub was owned and operated by a family named Hall; one visit convinced me they were no kin of mine. My only other trip to town came at Bill Colby's insistence; it was so cold at Dalnaglar that I'd let my hair grow to keep my brains from freezing solid. So did practically everyone else, and it finally reached the point where a person coming up behind the Norso Group would think he was overtaking a herd of yaks.

As the weather grew warmer—above twenty degrees—the Major ordered us to get haircuts. One of the men promptly claimed a knowledge of barbering and pulled a pair of scissors and some battered clippers out of his barracks bag to back it. He proved to be the kind who leaves nothing above the neck but ears, and maybe only one of them. I decided to take my chances in Blairgowrie. The barber there may or may not have been related to the shepherd, but I came back looking like a survivor of the Deerfield Massacre. From then on, most of us stuck with our comrade, and he eventually became passing fair.

During the second week in March, Bill Colby asked me to get a cup of coffee and come to his room after the evening meal. We were close friends, and he didn't waste any time on formalities.

"We've been alerted, I'm going to tell the others tonight, but first I have some news for you. The Norso Group has been split into two sections—I'm in command of the first, you're in command of the second. The operation will be in two phases. I'll take my unit in, then you bring yours in."

I stared at my cup and Bill knew what I was thinking.

"You're not being left behind and you're not being left

out of anything. Headquarters has decided to send half of us in at a time, there's much less chance of losing the whole group that way, and it also provides for reinforcements which may well be needed."

"Why me in command of the second section? Why not Sather?"

"You know Tom's the best skier we've got, besides being a Norwegian-American who speaks fluent German. Rocky's the best demolition man any of us will ever see, Blain's a good skier and has been with this bunch for more than a year. I have to leave one officer to command the second section. You're the logical choice."

"Swell."

"I don't expect you to like it, but I do expect you to understand. You can't ski, you missed a good deal of the training, and you're the junior officer in the group. I can't make it any plainer than that."

"You don't have to."

"You look as though someone stole your teddy bear."

"Don't know why I should, I ought to be used to this by now."

"You seem to be forgetting you will be coming into Norway. We'll need all the help we can get. The second section will come in much sooner than you think."

"If it comes in at all, it'll be much sooner than I'm thinking right now."

Later that evening, Colby gave all his officers a more detailed briefing.

"The drop will be on Lake Jaevso, east of Snassa in Nord-Tronderlag. It's frozen solid, and the underground will provide a reception party. I don't have to remind you how difficult the supply problem is. There'll be eight plane loads, each made up in self-contained units of men and supplies, each capable of independent operation in the field, on skis, for forty days without help, completely self-sufficient."

He went on, explaining details and issuing orders. When the briefing was over, he dismissed the others and gave me more explicit instructions regarding the second section.

"You'll stay here at Dalnaglar until I send for you. Keep up the mountain training routine, heavy on the weapons. The men are going to be bitched off about being assigned to the second section, don't give them a chance to grumble a morale problem into being. Work them so hard they won't have time to fret. You might be coming in at any time, so keep the section in top shape."

"I've been hearing about this second section all night. Who's in it, have you made up the roster yet?"

Major Colby hesitated a moment, nodded, and handed me a list.

"Here they are, twenty all told. I'll be taking thirty-three with me, plus the officers."

I read the names slowly. The second section was no more nor less than the second team.

"My compliments on your selections. With one exception those are the men I would have left behind."

"Who's the exception?"

"Sergeant Kyllo."

"As the supply sergeant, he'll be more valuable back here with the supplies."

"I guess that figures. When do you want me to tell the men they're being left to my tender mercies; at reveille?"

"No, you've been given enough of a headache. I'll explain things to the second section. And I wish you'd stop looking like that, you're coming to Norway too."

"When I do, what I'll bring with me will be the second section in name only."

The Group was divided the next morning into Norso-I and Norso-II, but it continued to train as a single unit. Most of the newly formed section realized that the men in Norso-I were the best skiers, and accepted that as the reason for the division. They didn't seem to be as perturbed about being left in reserve as they did about being left under my command. I'd been in charge of the daily run, which the men hated above all else in training, and Norso-II shuddered at the thought of what would happen when I took over the entire program.

The alert lasted for eight days, then the Air Corps finally reported suitable flying conditions, and Norso-I left Dalnaglar Castle to the accompaniment of raucous and not particularly envious farewells from Norso-II, which had been unofficially christened "The Mexican Militia."

I devoted the next week to making sure the men wished to God they had gone to Norway. An afternoon run and a second calisthenics period were added to the daily schedule, along with three unannounced night marches. Every weapon in the area was fired until it became too hot to hold, grenades were used up by the case, and each man made two consecutive bazooka hits or kept on shooting until he did. A reasonable facsimile of the Fort Benning tower jump was rigged up by running a cable from the roof of the castle to a tree on the far side of the lawn. The men thought this would be great fun until they found out the practice exits would be made at night with full operational equipment.

Colonel Bolland showed up at Dalnaglar ten days after Norso-I had left, bringing with him the first word we received on Operation Rype. One look at him and I knew it hadn't gone well; he didn't say anything, just handed me a brief official report:

"On the night of 24 March 1945, Major Colby, two officers, and eighteen men dropped on Jaevsjo Lake to a reception party. Eight planes started, four dropped at the target, one dropped personnel and loads in Sweden thinking it was over the target, three planes returned to the United Kingdom unsuccessful. On 31 March, a second try to get Norso-I in by air was made, all planes unsuccessful, one crashed in Orkney

Islands on the return trip, killing six of our personnel listed below. Copilot only survivor, he stated that two motors had failed on the Liberator bomber."

I read the names of those killed in the crash: Berge, Kjelness, Meland, Ottersland, Rorvick, Sondeno; for some reason I remembered that Johannes Rorvick came from Luck, Wisconsin.

"It's rough enough to lose six men, but that way! Have you heard from Major Colby?"

"Yes, he established and is maintaining daily radio contact. The drops were bad, men and equipment scattered, a good portion of the supplies lost because the container chutes hadn't been hooked up by the air crews."

"And a plane load dropped in Sweden besides. Norway's no dot on the map, it's a whole country. What the hell's the matter with the Air Force?"

The Colonel shook his head wearily before going on in his clipped, military manner of speaking.

"Inexperienced personnel, replacements. An investigation is underway."

"What happens now?"

"We're still trying to get Lieutenant Jones in with the remaining men and supplies. Major Colby is under orders to stay put until then."

"And Norso-II?"

"Continue training and await further orders."

The men were shaken by news of the crash. Almost all of them had come into the O.S.S. in a body from the 99th Mountain Battalion at Camp Hale, Colorado, and all told they had served together for more than three years. I had no choice but to work them even harder in an effort to keep their minds off it, and I had my hands full doing it. There was only one other officer at Dalnaglar Castle, the area commander, and he was generally regarded as feeble-minded.

There was incessant bitching, but both the morale and the

condition of Norso-II improved steadily, although my personal popularity didn't keep pace with either. A couple of the men were too tired one night to notice I was standing behind them in the chow line.

"The way the Lieutenant gallops around on the runs, the son-of-a-bitch must be half horse."

"You're right, and I know which half."

A week after Colonel Bolland's visit, I received a hurried phone call ordering me to report to London at once. Colonel Skabo was waiting for me, his face pale and drawn with strain.

"More bad news, Lieutenant. Another crash, no survivors. We lost Lieutenant Jones, Sergeant Anderson, Corporal Falck, and Corporal Iverson. Their plane hit a mountain eight kilometers from the target area. Major Colby was waiting, but they never came over."

He turned and looked out the window for what seemed a long time, then picked up some papers from his desk and began reading in a tired voice.

"Because of the repeated failures in getting Operation Rype into the field by air, 17 sorties flown 4 successful, and the short periods of darkness now becoming a hazard to flying that far north, this method is not to be used again."

He let the papers slip from his hand.

"Those are my orders. That leaves Colby in the field with two officers, eighteen men, and less than half his supplies. Here's what we're going to try and do. Colby has been ordered to begin attacking the Nordland Railway. Colonel Bolland will take the remainder of Norso-I by air to Sweden, then by courier to the operational area. Those six men made three attempts to get in by plane and parachute, maybe they'll make it on skis."

He sat down heavily before continuing.

"If Bolland can make it through Sweden, we'll try to send your group in the same way. That's the best I can offer you

now. Continue your present training program until further
orders. You can stay in London tonight if you wish, and return to Area 'P' tomorrow."

"Thank you, Colonel Skabo."

While I was putting on my trench coat, he started talking
again, but so softly it was difficult to hear.

"I asked them to send Rype in two months ago, and they
gave me the runaround about 'political considerations.' I
begged them for Norwegian pilots and British planes to fly
the sorties, they turned me down cold. I told them—"

His voice trailed off into silence. As I closed the door of
his office behind me, I realized how sorry I felt for the tired
old gentleman who was the commanding officer of Operation Rype.

I saw no point in keeping the unpleasant news from
Norso-II, they were beginning to develop a fatalistic attitude anyway and took it in stride. I eased up a bit on the
training program, after making it abundantly clear that the
reign of terror would be reinstated the moment the group
began to get sloppy. If by any miraculous chance we did get
sent into Norway via Sweden, which I doubted very much, it
would be in small units of not more than five men each, and
there would be weeks to prepare.

My plans for spending a relaxing spring in the Scottish
Highlands were rudely interrupted by a phone call from Mr.
Terry.

"Sorry your operation to Norway didn't come off, Roger."

"Well, there's always the C.B.I., although I'm sure the Japs
will quit the day I start their way."

"They might at that. I'm calling to let you know ahead of
time that we're sending you twenty Greeks."

"Bad connection, thought you said twenty Greeks."

"I did."

"Now what am I going to do with twenty Greeks?"

"Train them. We brought them all the way from the Mediterranean Theater to reinforce the Norso Group, they're all veterans of O.G. missions into Greece, mountain combat, good men. They arrived yesterday, and we can't keep them in London. They'll get to Perth tomorrow at noon."

"How many officers?"

"None, First Sergeant Strimenos is in command until you take over."

"I certainly do want to thank you, Mr. Terry, that's just what I need up here, twenty Greek O.G.'s and no officers. Now, if you could just arrange to have Dalnaglar Castle shelled some night—"

"Fine, Roger, fine. Call me anytime. Good-bye."

First Sergeant Strimenos, all six-feet-five and two hundred and forty pounds of him, brought his crew in on schedule. They were hard articles, and came complete with a set of jaw-breaking names. All except the one who looked more like a Greek than any of the others; his name was Brady.

I had had a few misgivings as to how the Norwegians and the Greeks would get along, but they hit it off fine from the start. I rearranged the training schedule on a competitive basis, pitting the two groups against each other in every conceivable manner. We even had map reading contests. It worked out beautifully.

Colonel Skabo came up and spent a few days at Dalnaglar Castle; he was feeling much better about things in general and Operation Rype in particular. Bill Colby had managed to recruit some Norwegian underground members in the field, and had somehow blasted the Tangen Bridge on the Nordland Railway in one raid, and three kilometers of rail in a second strike. He had successfully eluded all German patrols except one, which was promptly annihilated at the cost of only one Norso wounded. It also looked as though Colonel Bolland and his men would be able to get in by way of Sweden, and Colonel Skabo was optimistically predicting that Norso-II would follow soon. We were all aware, however, that we were rapidly running out of war.

Although things on the Continent were heading for a fast finish, there was still considerable speculation at Headquarters as to whether or not the crack German troops in Norway would make a last-ditch stand after the inevitable surrender of their High Command in Berlin. On the outside chance that they might, plans were made for prolonged operations in Norway, with Norso-II going in the moment the Germans caused trouble, followed by a full-scale Allied invasion.

With such an operation at least a possibility, I looked around for ways to keep the group sharp, and decided a jaunt through the British Parachute School would be just the thing. Colonel Skabo agreed, and the necessary orders were issued. Since the war in Europe was likely to end any day, the men took the news about more parachute training as proof positive that I had gone completely mad. There was no open mutiny, but remarks emanating from the mess hall, which was separated from the officers dining room by a thin partition, became even more uncomplimentary.

"He's nuts I tell you, a fruitcake in boots. Why would he do such a thing if he wasn't nuts?"

"Why not, it's his last chance to kill us."

Captain Peter Leghorn almost had a stroke when I descended on S.T.S. 51 with forty men of the unofficially rechristened Norgreek Group. Most of them had let their beards and hair grow, the barber having gone to Norway with Major Colby, and the resultant assemblage looked as though a band of Viking raiders had joined forces with Sicilian bandits. Leghorn gasped.

"Jesus deliver us from the Scourge of God and his Vandals."

"I am not Attila, and these fine young men are Norwegians and Greeks, not Huns."

"First Germans, now Norwegians and Greeks. What the

devil do you think I'm running here, an immigration center?"

On our last day at S.T.S. 51, I received orders from Colonel Skabo to bring the entire group back to London. When we arrived there, the twenty Greek-Americans were transferred out to await shipment back to the States. V.E. day was next, and Norso-II didn't get a chance to do any dancing in the streets. We were rushed back up to Area "P" under a twenty-four-hour operational alert. However, the Germans in Norway quit along with their comrades in Europe, and so we sat around Dalnaglar Castle and waited.

Colonel Skabo showed up early one morning with the news that Norso-II was flying to Norway the next day, and he was going with us. Norso-I had come down out of the mountains and gone to Namsos to bolster the Chief of Police because of the arrogant attitude of German Navy personnel there. Norso-II was to seize Vaernes Airfield, which was still occupied by German military personnel, and disarm a large number of S.S. troops who had gathered there. We all perked up at the news, it was more of a mission than any of us expected at this stage of the game.

Operation Better-Late-Than-Never took off in three B-24's, but the Air Force blew it again, and my plane was the only one that made it to Vaernes. Colonel Skabo's wound up 'way south of Oslo, and the third upheld tradition by landing in Sweden. This left me more firmly convinced than ever that most navigators were recruited from Giggle Tech.

When we jumped out onto the landing strip at Vaernes, the unused runways were packed with thousands of German troops. We were greeted by a reception committee of about a dozen Norwegian underground members.

Fortunately, one was an excellent interpreter, equally fluent in Norwegian, German, and English. Since Colonel Skabo wasn't around, I told the interpreter to stay close by and had a short chat with the chief of the local underground. He'd evidently been expecting at least a battalion of paratroopers, and seemed worried as he told me, "There are at least seven battalions of Germans here."

"I brought six men with me; we'll each take a battalion." That didn't do much good, so I added, "The five-man crew of my plane will be held in reserve."

He was in no mood for jokes, bad or otherwise. I couldn't think of anything else to do, so I decided to have the commander of each battalion surrender to me. I stood under a brace of machine guns in the nose turret of our B-24, and the gunner was on duty. The six Norso men were lined up behind me with the underground Norwegians. The German officers were instructed to come up, give their name, the military designation of their unit, and the number of men. It went smoothly enough at first. The Germans marched up one by one, clicked their heels and saluted, gave the required information, then wheeled and marched back to their units.

The fifth officer to do this wore one Iron Cross on a ribbon around his neck and another pinned over his heart. He was quite short, not much over five feet tall, walked with a bad limp, and had a powerful voice. After finishing the prescribed routine, he suddenly unsheathed his ceremonial dagger—all the officers were wearing them—and handed it to me hilt first, speaking loudly as he did. I heard my interpreter catch his breath.

"What did he say?" I asked.

"That he has been ordered to surrender, and as a soldier he must obey orders, but he and his men are like that blade and merely have been put in a sheath."

I looked at the hard features of the man standing rigidly in front of me, and wondered whether to let him have his moment. Then I remembered the Norwegians behind me and what they'd been through for five years. I bent over, placed the point of the dagger on the concrete, and stamped hard on the blade. It snapped. The German started to say something, then bit his lip, spun around, and limped back to his men. I heard a sigh from one of the Norso Group, and a tommy-gun bolt clicked forward slowly from the firing position.

The sixth German behaved himself, and as the seventh and last marched stiffly toward me, I caught sight of the double-lightning bolts on his collar that meant S.S. He was blond and good-looking, but he seemed young for the job. Before he said a word, the interpreter stepped forward and whispered in my ear.

"He's a lieutenant, the S.S. commander is a colonel."

"Ask him where the Colonel is."

The interpreter spoke, but there was no answer. The young officer grew red-faced and continued to stare straight ahead. The interpreter asked him twice more, and got the same results.

"Ask him if the Colonel is afraid of American soldiers."

He responded to that with an absolute torrent of words, and it was the interpreter's turn to redden.

"Give me an abridged version of it."

"The Colonel is in his quarters, he will surrender only to an officer of equal or higher rank. He will not surrender to a lieutenant."

"Where are his quarters?"

"There." He pointed to a group of houses on the edge of the field, about three hundred yards away.

"Give the Lieutenant a message for the Colonel. If the Colonel isn't out of there in fifteen minutes his quarters will be burned to the ground with phosphorus grenades."

The German Lieutenant raced off across the field. I glanced at my watch, then turned to the men behind me. The Norsos seemed primed and ready, but the Norwegian underground group were having an animated discussion, during which they kept giving me horrified looks. Their leader finally stepped forward.

"Lieutenant Hall, I much ask of you to give it the other thought about Colonel Stiefel."

"Why?"

"Sir, that is a fine house, please do not burn it."

"Besides," Sergeant Kyllo muttered, "we ain't got any phosphorus grenades." He had a point.

But it took Colonel Stiefel only about five minutes to arrive. He held out his hand, and said in heavily accented English.

"There has been an error, a mistakes, a—."

"Let's get on with it, Colonel."

The muscles in his face stood out as he stepped back, came to attention, and gave the necessary information. When he had finished, he saluted. I was under orders, issued by Headquarters, to neither shake hands with German officers nor return their salutes, so I turned abruptly and walked away after saying to the interpreter, "Tell them to stack all their weapons and ammunition in front of the middle hangar."

For the first time I noticed a group of about thirty civilians, many of them women and children, standing off to one side of the B-24. The underground leader motioned toward them.

"These people came from Hell to see you Americans."

"I hope it was worth the climb."

"Climb? From Hell to Vaernes is downhill."

Sergeant Kyllo straightened it out by explaining that Hell was a small town near the air field, and the Mayor would like to say a few words of welcome. It wasn't every day I received greetings from the Mayor of Hell, so I shook hands with the sturdy old gentleman, and listened as Kyllo interpreted his speech.

"This day means as much as the day the war ended, for

on this day the Americans come bringing freedom, and this
twentieth of May will live in our hearts—.'"

He went on for several minutes. When he had finished it
was my turn.

'Make out a guard-duty schedule for the plane," I said to
Kyllo. "I want a man here around the clock, use the crew
too. We'll take over the Colonel's quarters. Move our gear
and supplies in there. Tell that interpreter to move in too.
Supper at six-thirty, ten-in-one rations, invite the underground, we have plenty, and see if you can scrounge any
milk, but make sure it's pasteurized. Tell the radio operator
we'll want to send a message in an hour. Now pretend what
I've just told you is an answer to the Mayor's speech."

While the Sergeant spoke, I thought again about it being
the twentieth of May. It was my birthday—a birthday without a present, not even any good wishes. Kyllo finished.
There was a burst of applause, then a towheaded little girl
ran forward and handed me a bouquet of wildflowers.

Colonel Skabo arrived the next day and proceeded to put
the fear of God and the United States Army into every German for miles around. His first official visitor was Colonel
Stiefel, who complained bitterly that I had insulted him during the surrender proceedings. My Commanding Officer
couldn't have been more delighted, but his smile faded as
Stiefel said, "I demand an apol—"

Colonel Skabo's hand slammed down on his desk like the
crack of doom, and his eyes were blazing as he spat out the
words through clenched teeth.

"No German will demand anything for a long time."

There was one German Captain, however, who saw no
harm in asking. One of his more bizarre requests was for
me to help him get a job with American Airlines. He liked
to practice his English on me, usually in long-winded expla-

nations of how he had never been a Nazi. He seemed to be getting a bit hoarse one morning, so I interrupted.

"You served as an intelligence officer with the Luftwaffe for the last four years didn't you, Hauptmann Ott?"

"That is right, Lieutenant Hall."

"Tell me, did you ever hear of an outfit called the O.S.S.?"

"But certainly, the Office of Strategic Services, an American group. Very clever. We knew all about it."

"Really. What is it?"

"It is the cover story for a real intelligence organization."

A week later, Major Colby brought his men down from Namsos, and Norso-I and -II were reunited. The first section was in good shape and excellent spirits, although neither group could help but notice the gaps in our ranks at the first formation. Rocky told me about finding the plane in which Blain Jones and his men had been killed, and how they had been given a military burial in a raging blizzard with the mercury twenty below. (Eventually, these men were laid to rest in Cambridge, England, near their comrades who died in the Orkney Islands crash.)

The British rushed a military government unit to Vaernes, so Major Colby turned over command of the area to them and the Norso Group followed Colonel Skabo to Oslo. The Commander and Major Axel had also come to town, set up O.S.S. Headquarters in an overstuffed mansion, and were busy receiving the adulation of an uninformed public. The occupation was being handled jointly by an Anglo-Norwegian-U.S. combine of military and civil authorities, but the American commander didn't have much of a say in things.

Everyone was anxious to leave Norway, and getting back to London proved much less difficult than we feared it might be. The Norso Group left with the enthusiastic help of both the British and Norwegian armies; it embarrassed them to have Bill Colby and his men around while they were handing each other medals for being the first troops to land after the war was over.

We arrived back in London and found O.S.S. Headquarters almost stripped clean; the boys and girls had moved on to such spots as Paris, Brussels, Copenhagen, and Oslo. Fortunately, there was still enough of the crack Special Operations Branch administrative staff left to arrange our shipment back to the States, and we had priority orders at that. The Norso Group was appreciated by General Donovan and his staff, if by no one else, and was much in demand for operations in China.

FIFTEEN

the decline and fall of the O.S.S.

WE CAME back on the S.S. *Empire MacAndrews,* a baby flattop of the British Merchant Aircraft Carrier class. She had a load of P-51's on her flight deck, but there was still room to laze around. We had fine accommodations—staterooms for all—since there were only fifty officers and men in the shipment. The *Queen Mary* passed us as though we were drifting, but I knew how the boys were packed aboard her and didn't envy them a bit.

Our voyage took eleven days and got a bit monotonous in its latter stages because the ship's library left a great deal to be desired. When we began hearing commercials on the wireless, I knew the land of milk and hamburgers was near. Not a minute too soon though. Colby and I had been reduced to working jigsaw puzzles turned face down.

The length of the trip led to a rumor that we were headed for China, and on the morning of the eleventh day I was beginning to wonder myself. Everyone's mind was put to rest beautifully by the sight of a huge sign on the bluffs just outside Fort Hamilton which could be seen easily by any returning soldier, day or night, whether he came by air or sea. It read, "Welcome Home—Well Done."

We disembarked at Newark, then were taken straight to the Fort Hamilton mess hall and told to order anything we wanted. Fresh milk was the number-one request, and when the waiters brought additional quarts, Rocky groaned happily, "I can't drink another drop, throw it in my face!"

Next day we went down to Washington, and I almost fainted when someone from Headquarters met us at the station. He hustled us out to Area "F" in trucks; my old stamping grounds had been turned into a returnee reception center. It hadn't changed a bit, and Moose was waiting on the front steps.

We'd no sooner gotten settled than the staff started giving us tests, interviews, and physical exams, all with an eye to selecting the lucky ones who would go to China. Twenty-four hours later the atom bomb hit Nagasaki, and Colby remarked, "The next place we'll be going is into white shirts."

But first there was a thirty-day leave. I was in such a hurry to get to Annapolis—about forty-five miles from the area—that I put down my right address. Most of the others suddenly acquired residences in the Pacific Northwest, and were given additional travel time and allowances between there and Washington.

I wandered back from leave late, broke, and perfectly happy. They finally managed to reassemble enough of the Norso Group to have an awards ceremony, the highlight of which was the awarding of the Silver Star to Major William Colby.

The O.S.S., with no more war to play in, was flinging men back into the Army with an alarming vigor. I didn't particularly give a hoot, because I had enough points to get out and had been promoted to captain, but Moose saw to it that I was transferred to a newly created branch with the imposing title *Reports Declassification Section.*

As the hostilities came to an end, General Donovan began to have some well-founded fears about the continued existence of his baby. It had been tough enough when the shooting was taking place, and something drastic had to be done

if such carryings on were to be justified in peace time. He
and his advisers talked it over, the eventual decision being,
"Bring it out in the open, lift the cloak and show what the
dagger has done."

That was logical enough; it meant public recognition and
credit where it was due to the men and women agents, sabo-
teurs, and guerrilla fighters, living and dead, many of whom
had taken unbelievable risks.

So the Reports Declassification Section was created, its
function being to acquaint the American people with what
the O.S.S. had done, and, at the same time, keep within the
limits of military security. Commander John Shaheen, form-
erly a Chicago publicity man, was put in charge of the new
section.

From within the organization he recruited a staff of jour-
nalists, authors, photographers, and motion picture and radio
men, which he proceeded to shake well with a highly compe-
tent mixture of public relations and promotion experts. When
the section was ready to produce, the security lid which had
been so tightly locked down on everything the O.S.S. had
done since its inception was lifted. The story was told
through every information medium short of skywriting.

Most of it went out one of two ways: It was either written
in our offices and released to the press, or the writers came
in, were given access to the material, and then wrote stories
which had to be cleared by the section. Whenever possible,
pictures were furnished to illustrate the copy. Which is
where I came in. My assignment entailed seeing all the hitherto top-secret O.S.S. motion pictures and deciding what
could be clipped out and used for still shots in newspaper and
magazine articles.

"Deadline Johnny" Shaheen ran the place as though it
were straight out of *The Front Page.* The O.S.S. story was
the hottest thing in the news picture, the public was eating
it up and howling for more. Our offices swarmed with news-

men, magazine men, newsreel men, radio men, syndicated columnists, and free lancers, all crying for material and pictures. They got whatever it was possible to give them.

Only it didn't work. On October 1, 1945, the O.S.S. was abolished by a Presidential directive. The Reports Declassification Section stopped dead in its tracks. No more stories went out, no more scripts, no more interviews with heroes of guerrilla warfare, no more press luncheons for agents, no more access to the files, no more daily news releases, no more nothing. The sole remaining function of the section was to read and approve stories sent in for clearance, then send them over to the War Department for another clearance. The flower withered as quickly as it had bloomed.

When the O.S.S. folded, it was replaced by the S.S.U., the Strategic Services Unit of the War Department. The Reports Declassification Section was spared the *coup de grâce* longer than most. There still was material coming in which had to be read and cleared by someone who knew approximately what the score was, or at least who had played. I was offered the assignment and took it for two reasons: I didn't have anything else to do, and the idea of becoming a branch chief appealed to my baser nature.

It wore thin pretty quickly. The only bright spot was welcoming home various returning heroes. Erik the Great came storming in one day with a chestful of ribbons and some highly improbable stories of how he got them. Mills Brandies came right after Erik, then St. Legere, even Colonel Delano dropped by for a visit.

The Jedburghs who had gone to China straggled in; at least once a day the door would burst open and some long-unheard-but-still-familiar voice would roar, "There you are, right behind a desk just as I knew you'd be when I came back from battle!"

When most of the old crowd had come and gone, what little work there had been dwindled to the point where I stopped in at the nearest public library and brought a new book to the office every morning. Then came an incident which speeded my departure.

There was a large picture of General Donovan hanging on the wall behind my desk. Under it was a neatly lettered sign which read, "Our Founder."

I saw it the day I took over, thought it lent a nice touch to the place, and promptly forgot all about both the picture and the caption. One day while I was enjoying H. Allen Smith's latest literary effort, my secretary came in and announced, "A Mr. Cooley to see you."

He was from North Building, the sanctum sanctorum of the S.S.U. nee O.S.S., and had come down to see how things were going in the Reports Declassification Section. We had a pleasant chat, during which I told him I hadn't done a damn thing in weeks.

"Well, a lot of us find ourselves in that position these days, Captain Hall, but I think it best you stay around a bit longer. Never can tell what might come up."

Suddenly his voice became extremely chilly. "That's a nice picture of the General."

"Yes, a fine one. I intend to take it with me when I leave."

By then he was on his feet and stalking out the door. I turned and looked at the wall behind me. The picture was still there but some thoughtful soul had replaced the original caption with one which read, "WANTED."

I came in the next morning and found five large men moving all the furniture out of the office. They were followed by one who came to disconnect the phone. I held him at arms length long enough to sit on the floor, hum "Auld Lang Syne," and make one final call, the gist of which was, "My time has come."

It certainly had. The required orders were drawn up with what I felt was an almost unnecessary enthusiasm. I went through the routine of clearing a post, camp, or station—

neither the S.S.U. or O.S.S. being any of same—winced mentally when I told a quartermaster sergeant I didn't have any government equipment, then went over to the Pentagon and in two smooth-running days got myself separated from the Army. I also latched onto a large packet of terminal leave.

There was one thing left to do. I went back to "Q" Building, where I had signed in years before and started my ride on the merry-go-round. The same huge guard was on duty; we talked for a few moments, then I signed the officers register, put "Relieved from Active Duty" in the proper column, said, "So long, Tiny," and walked through the door.

It occurred to me that I should pay my respects to the Commanding Officer. I walked across the quadrangle, entered the North Building, went through two outer offices, and came to attention in front of General Donovan. He returned my salute with a smile, and said pleasantly, "Yes, Captain?"

"I'm leaving, sir. You'll have to go it alone from now on."

The Naval Institute Press is the book-publishing arm of the U.S. Naval Institute, a private, nonprofit, membership society for sea service professionals and others who share an interest in naval and maritime affairs. Established in 1873 at the U.S. Naval Academy in Annapolis, Maryland, where its offices remain today, the Naval Institute has members worldwide.

Members of the Naval Institute support the education programs of the society and receive the influential monthly magazine *Proceedings* and discounts on fine nautical prints and on ship and aircraft photos. They also have access to the transcripts of the Institute's Oral History Program and get discounted admission to any of the Institute-sponsored seminars offered around the country.

The Naval Institute also publishes *Naval History* magazine. This colorful bimonthly is filled with entertaining and thought-provoking articles, first-person reminiscences, and dramatic art and photography. Members receive a discount on *Naval History* subscriptions.

The Naval Institute's book-publishing program, begun in 1898 with basic guides to naval practices, has broadened its scope to include books of more general interest. Now the Naval Institute Press publishes about one hundred titles each year, ranging from how-to books on boating and navigation to battle histories, biographies, ship and aircraft guides, and novels. Institute members receive significant discounts on the Press's more than eight hundred books in print.

Full-time students are eligible for special half-price membership rates. Life memberships are also available.

For a free catalog describing Naval Institute Press books currently available, and for further information about subscribing to *Naval History* magazine or about joining the U.S. Naval Institute, please write to:

Membership Department
U.S. Naval Institute
291 Wood Road
Annapolis, MD 21402-5034
Telephone: (800) 233-8764
Fax: (410) 269-7940
Web address: www.navalinstitute.org